Paradigm Shifts in Management Theory

Paradigm Shifts in Management Theory is an illuminating exploration of the evolving landscape of management science. This book goes beyond the surface, delving into profound insights and perspectives that redefine traditional paradigms.

Through rigorous analysis and reflective narratives, each chapter unveils the transformative shifts shaping organizational leadership, offering a comprehensive understanding of key concepts and methodologies. From classical principles to emerging paradigms, elucidating the future of organizational leadership, readers will gain invaluable insights through empirical evidence and theoretical explorations, fostering a nuanced comprehension of practical applications. Advanced students, researchers, and practitioners will find that this book equips readers with essential knowledge to navigate the complexities of modern management science, fostering critical thinking and innovative approaches in real-world scenarios. Practitioners in organizational leadership benefit from practical insights and innovative perspectives, enhancing strategic decision-making and competitive advantage. Additionally, policymakers and interdisciplinary scholars exploring social phenomena find value in the interdisciplinary exchange facilitated by paradigm shifts. Embracing these shifts is crucial for advancing management science, ensuring its relevance and effectiveness in addressing contemporary challenges.

Catering to a diverse audience within academia and professional settings, it serves students and researchers in management studies, offering a robust foundation in theoretical frameworks and research methodologies.

Łukasz Sułkowski is Professor and Head of the Department of Management of Higher Education Institutions at Jagiellonian University, Cracow, Poland; President of PCG Poland; and President of Academy WSB in Dabrowa Gornicza, Poland.

Regina Lenart-Gansiniec is a Professor in the Department of Management of Higher Education Institutions at Jagiellonian University, Cracow, Poland.

Routledge Advances in Management and Business Studies

Entrepreneurship in the BRICS
Economic Development and Growth in the Post-Pandemic World
Edited by Ndivhuho Tshikovhi, Fulufhelo Netswera and Ravinder Rena

Start-up Strategy and Entrepreneurial Development
Evolving Business Models and Economic Trends
Edited by Iwona Skalna and Aleksandra Gąsior

Enterprise Risk Management
Technical, Cognitive, and Social Perspectives
Mirna Jabbour and Jason Crawford

Navigating the Ecological Transition
A Business School Perspective
Edited by Hugues Bouthinon-Dumas, Arijit Chatterjee and Bernard Leca

Regional Climate Leadership in East Asia and the Pacific
Kate Crowley and Akihiro Nakamura

Entrepreneurship in the Creative Industries
Contemporary Perspectives from the Arabian Gulf and Asia
Edited by Naveed Yasin

The Mechanisms of Agile Management
Klara-Aylin Wenten

Paradigm Shifts in Management Theory
Łukasz Sułkowski and Regina Lenart-Gansiniec

For more information about this series, please visit: www.routledge.com/Routledge-Advances-in-Management-and-Business-Studies/book-series/SE0305

Paradigm Shifts in Management Theory

Łukasz Sułkowski and
Regina Lenart-Gansiniec

Routledge
Taylor & Francis Group
NEW YORK AND LONDON

First published 2025
by Routledge
605 Third Avenue, New York, NY 10158

and by Routledge
4 Park Square, Milton Park, Abingdon, Oxon, OX14 4RN

Routledge is an imprint of the Taylor & Francis Group, an informa business

ISBN: 9781032866345 (hbk)
ISBN: 9781032871028 (pbk)
ISBN: 9781003530947 (ebk)

DOI: 10.4324/9781003530947

Typeset in Times New Roman
by codeMantra

Contents

Tables

Introduction

Research by Kuhn found that knowledge building in science is a process marked by occasional great lurches forward, which he called 'paradigms'. According to Kuhn, a paradigm is a universally recognized scientific achievement that, over a period of time, provides model problems and solutions. It includes common postulates related to the nature of organizational reality and ways of challenging it, criteria regarding scientific truth, the attitude to values, identification of the researcher, and the attitude to management practice. One may be tempted to say that a paradigm is a valid worldview, a way of seeing the world.

In today's world, the functioning of organizations is determined by fundamental changes, often forced upon the organization by the environment or growing customer expectations. This implies the need for a radical change not only in management practice but also in theory. For management practice, this primarily means the need to look for new ways to build and maintain a competitive advantage. For theory, the need for change makes it insufficient for the functioning of organizations to be viewed from the perspective of just one paradigm. As a result, new positions or approaches appear.

Paradigm shifts in management science are linked to significant changes in the basic frameworks, assumptions, and methodologies related to studying social phenomena. These changes usually appear when the dominating paradigms are shown to be insufficient in explaining new concepts or empirical discoveries or when alternative theoretical viewpoints grow in importance. Such changes bring with them implications for creating scientific knowledge based on existing research methodologies. This is accompanied by changes in the way researchers conduct the conceptualization, operationalization, study, and interpretation of social concepts or phenomena.

A shift in paradigms intensifies the reassessment of current knowledge, established theories, concepts, and methodologies in a given field. Researchers focus on examining current knowledge and redefining the existing understanding of social phenomena. This process can include revision or rejection of previously accepted theories and the emergence of new theoretical frameworks.

DOI: 10.4324/9781003530947-1

Consequently, paradigm shifts drive progress and improvement in the state of knowledge about management science.

What is more, paradigm shifts can foster interdisciplinary cooperation and the integration of different points of view. New emerging paradigms may extend beyond the borders of individual disciplines, fostering the exchange of ideas, theories, and methodologies between disciplines. This most certainly helps to enrich the collective state of knowledge about management science. Additionally, paradigm shifts promote the inclusion of various voices and perspectives, questioning the domination of certain viewpoints and supporting a more inclusive understanding of social phenomena. Lastly, paradigm shifts in management science have an important influence and far-reaching impact both on the creation of scientific knowledge and on research methodology. They induce a critical reassessment of existing theories and methodologies and facilitate the emergence of new scientific knowledge. These changes also affect research practice, guiding the selection and application of research methodologies. In addition, they stimulate interdisciplinary cooperation and the inclusion of various perspectives. What is more, adopting paradigm shifts is key to the development of management science, ensuring its accuracy and methodological rigor in understanding and resolving complex social phenomena.

Additionally, paradigm shifts often accelerate changes in management science. Alongside the emergence of new theoretical perspectives, researchers can adopt alternative research methods and techniques in accordance with the new paradigm. Researchers can also make use of new tools and technologies for gathering and analyzing data, thereby facilitating innovative research.

However, despite the many potential benefits stemming from paradigm shifts, their implementation poses a considerable challenge due to possible unwillingness or resistance among researchers with regard to the changes. Such resistance can complicate the adoption of new paradigms and hamper progress in generating knowledge. Importantly, overcoming such resistance requires the researcher to reassess their beliefs, assumptions, and research methodologies.

This book is divided into 14 chapters forming three parts dedicated to the theoretical approach to paradigms, the re-evaluation of current paradigms in management science, and a practical new approach to paradigms in management science. Each chapter is prepared in such a way as to allow the reader to find their own point of reference as well as inspiration for their theoretical considerations and empirical research. The reference literature at the end of each part aims to provide the reader with points of reference and also directions for further methodological investigations.

The first part comprises four chapters. In Part I, readers are invited to embark on a journey of discovery, laying the groundwork for deeper exploration into the transformative power of paradigm shifts in management science.

In Part II, we embark on a journey of critical inquiry and deep reflection, as we re-evaluate the existing paradigms that shape the landscape of management science. By fostering a deeper understanding of the dynamics of paradigm shifts, this section aims to pave the way for innovation and progress within the field of management science.

In the third and final part, we transition from theoretical exploration to practical application, unveiling innovative approaches informed by paradigm shifts in management science. Through this practical exploration, readers will gain actionable insights and innovative strategies for navigating paradigm shifts in management science. By embracing new approaches and reimagining traditional practices, organizations can thrive in an ever-changing business landscape.

The book *Paradigm Shifts in Management Theory* is a comprehensive exploration of the multifaceted challenges and ethical dilemmas encountered in the realm of management science.

- Academic scholars navigating the complex realm of management science theories often find themselves amidst a sea of practicality, where the emphasis on applicability creates a cacophony of information. In this chaotic landscape, researchers yearn for criteria rooted in scientific knowledge to bring order to their specific observations. As such, the epistemological and theoretical sections of the book hold particular appeal for these scholars;
- Postgraduate researchers seeking validation for their conceptual choices in research and analysis endeavors will find solace in the clear justifications provided within the methodological portion of the book. This section serves as a beacon of guidance for those embarking on scholarly pursuits, whether in articles, monographs, or other academic endeavors;
- While the book's format and structure may not align seamlessly with the needs of students in management science, who often seek more tangible connections between theoretical frameworks and practical applications, it holds promise for PhD students, and certain segments may resonate with MBA students;
- For practitioners in the field of management science who grapple with an abundance of case studies and trendy buzzwords, the methodological and method-focused sections of the book offer valuable insights;
- Moreover, delving into the theoretical aspects may provide practitioners with a deeper understanding of the foundations underlying their day-to-day practices.

This book transcends the surface-level understanding of management science, inviting readers to embark on a journey of discovery and enlightenment. With a blend of rigorous analysis and thought-provoking reflections, each chapter presents a nuanced examination of key concepts, theories, and methodologies in management science. From classical principles to contemporary methodologies, this book embarks on a journey of discovery, illuminating the emergent paradigms that shape the future of organizational leadership. Through insightful analysis and empirical evidence, it unravels the complexities of management theory, offering invaluable insights into its practical applications. Whether you are a student, researcher, or practitioner, this book provides valuable perspectives on the multifaceted realm of management science, paving the way for a deeper understanding and application in real-world contexts.

Part I

Theoretical Approach to Paradigms in Management Science

1 Basics of Management Science

In managing, we want others to function in accordance with our assumptions. Thanks to management, rational individuals can achieve their goals. The exercising of power is related not only to the possibility of applying pressure (rewards, sanctions) but also to forms of 'symbolic violence' (Bourdieu 1987, pp. 147–166). Power can also be exercised very subtly, and by using the authority of science or social groups (such as the family), as well as valuing and subjecting to assessment (Becker 2003), it can assume more or less camouflaged forms. Cohesion can be achieved thanks to the mechanisms of power, enabling the creation of a coercive organization – united through coercion, 'negative power', or an integrative organization that is the effect of consensus, that is 'positive' or 'symbolic power' (Dahredorf 1969, p. 159). In a factual sense, the organization is a collection of fields of power and interest groups competing for them. Considering management as a process of exercising power provides new opportunities for explaining management processes as well as organizational culture, structure, and strategy. Fields of research on the border between management and sociology also include micropower, legitimization, authority, leadership, and the previously mentioned symbolic violence (Dixon, Dogan 2002).

Many definitions emphasize the organization of people's work in such a way that the collective entity – the organization – can achieve its designated goals (Bhatt 2001). While a manager manages processes or projects, management is often identified with the whole organization or its functional division. Within classical management discourse, people management in the organization is found among the concepts of leadership functions (Carroll, Gillen 1987, pp. 38–51). From an administrative perspective, managing people's actions consists of the processes of planning, organization, coordination, leadership, and control (Donaldson, Fafaliou 2007, pp. 297–309).

Interpreted in this way, management draws inspiration from mathematical, sociological, and psychological theory. The psychological and social conditions for decisions comprise both rational and irrational motives for action. Concepts regarding the rational choice of strategy make use of game theory and knowledge

DOI: 10.4324/9781003530947-3

management concepts (Pintelon, Gelders 1992; Barney 1995; Holsapple 1995; Abubakar et al. 2019).

Management can be treated as a series of decisions taken in order to achieve the organization's goals (Daellenbach, McNickle, Dye 2012). This is a teleological and multidimensional process, usually supported nowadays by information technology and increasingly using AI methods (Shankaranarayanan, Cai 2006). Although the essence naturally remains the taking of decisions, also taken into account are the aims, motives, and values of decision-makers and stakeholders, in addition to obtaining and processing reliable information. The choice of a given variant by management changes the functioning of the organization. Exerting influence, exercising power, and communication, as well as learning – none of this can take place without a prior act of will – making a decision. At the core of management are rational actions – which brings this science closer to the assumptions of *homo oeconomicus*, as the epistemological basis for classical economic sciences. In organization theory, increasing importance is placed on linking the goals of actions, and even rationality criteria, with values (Papadakis, Lioukas, Chambers 1998).

In management, there is also discussion on the limitation of decision-making rationality due to the limits of the human cognitive apparatus or access to information as well as due to socio-cultural conditions (Brunson 2007). The acting entity must be understood in a social, market, and also biological context (Pritchard 2002). If we do not have at our disposal universal criteria for truth and rationality, we must assume that socially established values guide cognition. Such axiological entanglement leads not only to correcting the *homo oeconomicus* model and consent for the assumptions of limited rationality (Simon 1978) but also to questioning the hyperrational approach in management (Soelberg 1966). For example, the concepts narcissistic leadership, the management of meaning, decision-making irrationality (Brunson 2006), and tacit knowledge and intuition do not bring the motivations for a person's actions within the organization exclusively down to the sphere of rationality. In other trends, the subjective understanding of interests, perceptions, and limiting the information horizon is also built in to the decision-making model.

The systems management concept originates in the systems paradigm, one of the most important ways of defining the organization (Khorasani, Almasifard 2017). Here, the management process involves striving for balance, thanks to which beneficial effects can be achieved in the exchange and processing of organizational resources (Cigoli, Scabini 2012).

Resources are basic assets absorbed from the environment thanks to which the organization functions. We can distinguish such resources as human, knowledge, financial, technical, and natural (Aldag, Stearns 1995). Management is a set of actions directed towards the organization's resources and undertaken with the intention of efficiently achieving its goals. Understood praxeologically, efficiency is the ability to undertake both individual and group actions and their effectiveness, not limited only to economic efficiency. Management makes the achievement of the organization's goals possible thanks to the processes of coordination, integration, transformation, and the efficient use of resources. If we treat management as "regulating the flow of resources thanks to taking decisions aimed at achieving the organization's goals", we see elements of the three ways of understanding this basic concept, as discussed above. The configuration of organizational resources is connected to ensuring a competitive advantage.

The choice of the way of perceiving the management process brings with it epistemological consequences. Some simplification is brought by looking from the social and economic point of view. From an economic perspective, management is the taking of decisions and the flow of resources. This uses the assumptions of limited rationality and the desire to preserve the functional balance of the organizational system. From a social perspective, management is perceived through the processes of the distribution of power and cultural patterns and values, not extending beyond the canon of economic rationality and leading to a socially constructed organization – in the interactions of organizational actors. If we risk stating that these concepts are complementary, then management science will be their synthesis.

To sum up, 'management' creates a 'word family', that is the foundation for the epistemological, methodological, and institutional development of the scientific discipline. The concept has several different historically variable and culturally relativized semantic roots. Apart from those described above, we can also enumerate other examples: management as leadership, a project or a process, including the process of social stratification. I think we have managed to show that it is a concept with multiple meanings that is open and created socially. However, it should be remembered that it is not a completely contradictory or blurred concept. The differences between paradigms and management schools do not exclude the existence of a limited field of consensus among researchers and practitioners. Common points within management include purposeful organizational action that occurs as a result of taking decisions and exercising managerial authority.

2 How Creating Knowledge in Management Science

Every researcher should partake in reflection on four questions: How is theory in management understood? How do we distinguish types of theory? How are theories created in management science? How is the cognitive usefulness of theories verified? D.A. Gioia and E. Pitre claim that theory is the coherent description, explanation, and presentation of experienced phenomena (Gioia, Pitre 1990). Scientific theory therefore comprises logical, consistent, and nonconflicting generalizations created on the basis of scientific knowledge. Important features of theory, which also apply to management science, include:

- Drawing conclusions from scientific facts (inductive and deductive);
- Cumulation of scientific achievements;
- Logical inference and consistency;
- Consistency between the paradigm, methodology, and research issues.

Management science (like other social sciences) is not able to fulfil the rigorous requirements regarding theory, such as verificationism in reaching the truth, mathematical formalism in describing reality, or complete coherence with previously gathered scientific knowledge (Bacharach 1989; Alvesson 2003; Goldman 2016).

The theory was fundamentalistically defined by the metamathematics program of D. Hilbert. This manner of pursuing science was adopted by the neopositivists of the Vienna Circle. However, criticism of neopositivism in the social sciences encourages the adoption of a more cognitively open position with regard to scientific theory (Mancosu 1998; Johnson, Duberley 2015, pp. 760–776).

Management expects consistent and logical theories rooted in scientific facts but able to make use of various paradigms, on the basis of which there is a cumulation of scientific achievements. The transfer of knowledge between paradigms is not always straightforward due to their disparity. A cumulation of knowledge comes about, but it cannot be said to be fully coherent. Management science cannot therefore be subject to the same methodological rigor as the natural sciences (Longino 2001). It is not possible to directly translate management theories into mathematical models, and it is difficult to reproduce them in the

DOI: 10.4324/9781003530947-4

language of mathematical logic. In addition, they are not used to formulate laws but historically and socially limited generalizations (Schmitt 1994). These are not universal but are culturally relativized, are subject to fashion, and are created according to various conventions, while their reach is limited.

Theorizing does not constitute a synonym for creating scientific theory as its meaning is broader. It assumes not only the creation of theory but also the undertaking of theoretical reflection in general, without assuming ultimate success in the form of a theory. In management, many levels of theorizing can be distinguished as well as categorized according to generality. The philosophy of management consists of general assumptions that we find in the concepts of authors such as P. Drucker, F.W. Taylor, H. Fayol, and M.P. Follet as well as the creators of subdisciplines of management such as Ph. Kotler and I. Ansoff. Meanwhile, management paradigms constitute cognitive assumptions related to the way a given scientific discipline is pursued among researchers representing a scientific school (which is an institutional reflection of the paradigm in the scientific community). Irrespective of the level of theorizing, the research community is based on certain shared cognitive assumptions, which T. Kuhn calls a paradigm (Kuhn 2012). Theorizing therefore encompasses not only the creation of theory but also its testing.

How are theories in the social sciences divided up? There are a great many options, whether by scope (micro, mezzo, macro), structure (tightly and loosely connected systems of thought), or course (dynamic or static processes). In terms of scope, in management science we find the most theories of average scope as well as microtheories, for course – analysis of dynamic processes – and for structure – loose systems of thought.

The division of theory into levels has its origin in R.K. Merton's concept of scope as well as in the dichotomy of the scope division of theories by D. Easton. Macrotheories are characterized by a high degree of generalization and high predictive power (long range theories) and are most frequently found in physics and in the natural sciences in general. Also in the social sciences, some functionalistic theories refer to the social system as a whole, although it is difficult to carry out their potential falsification (e.g. systems theory) because they are speculative. Attempts to build a macrotheory in management include strategic management, systems theories of organization, and functionalistic management theories. Most often it ends at these attempts; as similarly to economics, management adapts macrotheories from other sciences. Examples include behavioural economics (from cognitive and evolutionary psychology) and decision-making theories (from cognitive psychology). Theories of average scope (mezzo theories) only propose generalizations, which are limited by social and historical conditions but which can be verified according to the assumptions of neopositivism. In management, such theories relate to various areas of the functioning of the enterprise. Microtheories are used in the analysis of individual cases and are useful in making sense of the studied processes, without seeking generalizations.

In the interpretive trend, the micro level has been achieved by theories linked to organizational strategy and organizational culture. The level of theorizing largely depends on the adopted paradigm. The functionalist approach seeks to create a macrotheory or at least a theory of average scope. Interpretivism remains at the microtheory level. The critical trend theorizes at all three levels and postmodernism at none of them.

Operating on the basis of functionalism, T. Parsons and E.A. Shils are the authors of the division of theories in the social sciences, which takes into consideration a combination of the most important classification criteria, that is the scope, function, and structure. Four types of theory are therefore assumed (the order here indicates the generality): *ad hoc* theories, taxonomies, conceptual structures, and theoretical systems (Table 2.1).

The theory building process is either cyclical or linear. In the linear model, it moves from the conceptualization phase to the testing and verification phase, which completes the process of forming a given theory. In the circular model, the creative cycles are repeated in order to describe reality ever more precisely. This model would seem to be more appropriate for management.

Table 2.1 Types of theory in the social sciences

Theory type	*Characteristic*	*Example*
Ad hoc	Conventional arrangement of facts according to accepted categories not rooted in a more general theory of organization and management	Analysis of organizational cultures based on dichotomies (strong and weak or positive and negative culture)
Taxonomies	Schemas enabling the organizing of observations, describing the dependencies between categories. The categorization systems reflect reality	Typologies of authors such as Ch. Handy, T. Deal, A. Kennedy
Conceptual structures	Theorem system logically connected to descriptive and empirical categories. This is the next stage in the development of theory, enabling not only the arrangement and demonstration of the dependencies between categories but also an explanation	Concept of identity dynamics by M.J. Hatch and M.S. Schultz
Theoretical systems	The most advanced stage: sets of theorems, deductive systems, taxonomies, and conceptual structures allowing for explanation and prediction	Difficult to indicate systems *sensu stricto*

Source: Own elaboration on the basis of: Deal and Kennedy (1982); Handy (1985); Hatch and Schultz (2000, pp. 24–25).

R. Dubin distinguished eight components of scientific theory, which at the same time constitute phases in the creation of theory. These are:

1 Defining the units of theory – the basic elements that form relationships in the process being examined;
2 Describing the relations and principles on which the relationships between theory units are based;
3 Defining the theory boundaries, allowing for (a) focusing the process of explaining reality on key forces and relationships and (b) demarcation from other theories;
4 Defining the system state – how does the system function under the influence of specific forces, and what relationships occur between theory units;
5 Proposing a theoretical model completely describing cause and effect relationships;
6 Operationalization of the model, that is finding empirical indicators that can be measured and tested;
7 Posing hypotheses or research questions, thanks to which it will be possible to determine the status of empirical indicators during the testing process;
8 Testing, that is verification of the hypotheses or an attempt to answer the research questions posed (Dubin 1983, pp. 17–39).

The theory forming process is not possible without testing and thus also conducting research. The pragmatic stages in creating management theory can, in simple form, be depicted as a cycle of theorizing and concept testing during research:

1 Outlining the research field and problem;
2 Indicating the level of theory;
3 Identifying the paradigm;
4 Analysing the theories and research related to the problem;
5 Posing research questions, theses, or hypotheses;
6 Selecting the methodology for the paradigm, theory, and research problem;
7 Conducting the research;
8 Interpreting the results and drawing conclusions;
9 Analysing, correcting, and then accepting or rejecting the theory;
10 Defining a new research field and problems as a consequence of the theory.

The principal differentiation in building theory takes into account the division into inductive and deductive strategies. However, research practice in management science has shown that a mixed inductive-deductive strategy is usually applied, also referred to as pragmatic abduction in philosophy (Mitchell 2018; Philipsen 2018). This usually leads from the researcher's experiments and their results to attempts at initial generalizations, without falsification processes, then to selective gathering of facts using the inductive method, and finally to the formulation of frameworks for the deductive theory, which is corrected to form a full theory thanks to the use of continuously conducted research designed for this purpose.

The selection of research strategy and the building of theory is dependent on the paradigms adopted by the researcher. The prevailing division here is into theories of the dominant paradigm (functionalism, neopositivism, systems theory) and alternative theories (interpretivism, critical trend) (see Table 2.2).

Strategies for constructing theory are situated on a continuum and consist of theories based on the dominant paradigm and alternative theories. We can therefore distinguish four strategies: functionalism, interpretivism, epistemological pluralism, and epistemological eclecticism.

In 'pure functionalism', the assumptions of a functionalist-neopositivist-systems paradigm are taken into account when creating theories and research methodology. Starting with induction, the researcher poses hypotheses which they then verify using the adopted method. It is also possible to begin with deduction, which requires the assumption of a specific cognitive structure that is subject to verification or falsification through hypotheses and research. In this case, quantitative methods are the most frequently used research methods.

'Pure interpretivism' uses individual, in-depth organizational studies or comparative analyses. The task is not to verify hypotheses but to seek the meaning behind the behaviours of people in the organization. The aim is not to achieve one consistent picture; conflicting approaches and interpretations are often

Table 2.2 Dominant and alternative paradigms

Criteria	*Dominant paradigm*	*Alternative paradigms*
Relations between elements of reality	Cause and effect Recurrent	Interdependencies Recurrent and individual
Research aims	Generalization Verification Analysis, prediction, and programming changes	Comprehension Description Synthesis Stimulating change
Researcher's relationship to reality	Objective External viewpoint (*outsider*)	Participant in the studied phenomena and processes (*insider*)
Researcher's relationship to values	Striving for objective cognition, without evaluation	Awareness of being entangled in values (axiological position)
Preferred methodology	Explanatory – providing predictions based on abstract concept systems	Descriptive – explanatory or comprehending (hermeneutical)
Preferred methods	Standardized, quantitative, and structured methods	Non-standardized, qualitative, and unstructured methods

Source: Own elaboration on the basis of: Swedberg (1990).

presented depending on the social actors. Here, use is predominantly made of qualitative methods.

'Epistemological pluralism', similarly to the '10:00 approach' by K. Weick, combines approaches from various paradigms but at the same time strives to achieve consistent cognitive results. The interpretation of research is circular in nature (Weick 1979) and uses Ch. S. Pierce's assumptions of abduction. Use can be made of functionalist concepts (hypotheses, verification, or falsification), interpretative concepts (meaning, interpretation), or critical concepts (false awareness). The aim of the research methodology is complementarity (methodological triangulation) and the synthesis of quantitative and qualitative methods, also including engaged methods.

In management science, theory is created on the basis of various paradigms, which is why it finds itself in the state of temporary or permanent 'multi-paradigmaticity'. Although the functionalist-neopositivist approach dominates (with the assumptions: falsificationism and objectivism), there are also alternative paradigms with interpretative theories in circulation. Such tension within the discipline can also be found in other social sciences, but here the dualism is underlined by the very strong linkage with management practice. Managers appear to trust neopositivist management tools, but practice often gives a voice to interpretive and constructivist pragmatic methods. In alternative paradigms, management theory often constitutes conventional constructs used for setting the organizational reality in order (marketing-mix, M.E. Porter's sector model and G. Hofstede's 'onion' model of organizational culture), while thanks to tools, management cognizes and changes the world. Management theories cannot therefore be limited to one paradigm, which leads to epistemological pluralism. In formulating management theory, it is necessary to use conceptual apparatus from various paradigms. It is not possible to conduct research without research questions, theses or hypotheses, and research methodology, but it is also worth trying qualitative methodology, interpretation, discourse, and reflexive and critical analysis. Constructing theory, as a creative enterprise, requires knowledge and reflection. It also turns out to be helpful to adopt a non-orthodox position, to make use of induction, deduction, and abduction, and to reach for epistemological pluralism. A qualitative research approach adopting the assumptions of reflexivity, criticism, and creativity can sometimes be defined more as an inquiry than research.

Many management science concepts are scientific theories, however not in the understanding of the natural sciences – they are characterized by a considerably lower degree of generality and a weaker predictive power. They also do not contain broader use of a mathematical apparatus. However, can we say that the short scope of management science theories is unequivocal proof of their un-scientificness? (Pfeffer 2007). Neopositivists would answer in the affirmative, as for them there can be no ideal of 'real' science without verification or falsification and measurement. Viewed in this way, management that leads to perfecting the organization would exclusively constitute a practical, non-scientific activity. The theoretical and methodological analyses conducted within the scope of management science bring it closer to metaphysics, not science. Such neopositivist assumptions constitute a source of complexes for some researchers – in comparison to technical or natural science fields. However, management fulfils the criteria of scientificity as a practical, cognitive, and culture-forming activity, subject to content and methodological rules. It also addresses key contemporary problems of effective organization, creating medium-range theories, modifying social reality and functioning within academic institutions. It is therefore interpreted as a science, performing cognitive functions systematized by method.

3 Current Paradigms in Management Science

If we wish to fit the development of management science to Kuhn's model, we must decide if our discourse is used within a given paradigm and not always only one. The majority of researchers consider management to be a multi-paradigmatic science, although many representatives of the dominant trend proclaim the superiority of one particular paradigm. Meanwhile, according to some postmodernists, we are in a permanent post-paradigmatic state (Clegg, Hardy 1997, pp. 5–17; Hassard, Wolfram Cox 2013, pp. 1701–1728).

The classification of paradigms is not uniform (Donaldson 1995). The oldest typologies refer to management schools or trends. The chronology of several schools may be noted, usually occurring periodically and also synchronously (Laszlo, Waddock, Sroufe 2017). The first stage is pre-paradigmatic, in which many approaches to the cognitive issues are mixed together, and specialists have not yet come to agreement on the fundamental cognitive issues. Following this, the collected theoretical and empirical achievements become an extension of the dominant paradigm (a state of 'normality') (Ewoldsen 2017, pp. 1–17). Naturally, certain anomalies appear that are hard to interpret and which lead to a crisis of the paradigm and the emergence of competing theories (an 'abnormal' state). There may be a schism among researchers – some will follow the new theory, while others will remain supporters of the existing theory. If the terminology does not overlap, we are faced with the incommensurability of the theories. After a certain time, however, a new more general paradigm is created (again a state of 'normality') (Doppelt 2013, pp. 43–51). The cycles demonstrate the discontinuous development of science.

This attempt to set in order the development stages is conventional and incomplete in nature. Further trends may come into existence at the same time but generally do not become paradigms. Management may find itself only at the pre-paradigmatic stage, in expectation of the emergence of a dominant approach (Sapru 2008). This may imply a long-term perspective, as it took scientists many centuries to pass through the pre-paradigmatic stage. However, will a new paradigm actually emerge? Or is a feature the very lack of a paradigm? Adoption of this interpretation would seem to be prompted by the experiences of social

DOI: 10.4324/9781003530947-5

sciences with a longer tradition than management, such as economics, sociology, and psychology. Management may only allow for the building of medium- and short-range theories and not theories in the meaning of the exact sciences. Will it however ever enter the stage of creating long-range theories?

1 Management will integrate with other scientific fields, and organizational processes will be captured in mathematical models that can be translated into psychosocial processes. This assumes the existence of one universal fundamental paradigm, common to the natural and social sciences. One example is the paradigm of evolution, which is common to biology, psychology, and behavioural economics. This is a monistic, reductionist position (rooted in the neopositivist thesis of the unity of science and the emergence of subsequent ontological levels).
2 Management has specific features that differ from those of the natural sciences but are characteristic for social sciences. A universal common paradigm for social and/or humanistic sciences will emerge. This is a dualistic position (assuming the distinctness of reality in the social and natural sciences and supported by W. Dilthey, F. Tönnis, and M. Weber).
3 A paradigm will come into being that is specific for management, thanks to which the science will attain a state of 'normality'. However, this would seem to be less likely due to the number of paradigms that extend beyond our discipline (such as Neopositivist-functionalist-systems (NFS), Critical Management Studies (CMS), and IS).
4 Management will remain in a multi-paradigmatic state in which concepts and methods based on incommensurable cognitive assumptions will co-exist within various trends.

In the literature, we can find a great many proposals for differentiating paradigms in the social sciences. Seven of them are worth enumerating:

1 Subject division (according to the subdisciplines of management science);
2 Management schools from a chronological perspective (e.g. according to M. Bielski);
3 Paradigms of the social sciences according to the division by G. Burrell and G. Morgan;
4 Management paradigms according to M.J. Hatch;
5 Epistemologies of management research according to P. Johnson and J. Duberly;
6 Cognitive frameworks for understanding the organization according to L.G. Bolman and T.E. Deal;
7 G. Morgan's organization metaphors.

The classification of paradigms in management science is an extremely difficult task due to the number of proposals and the ambiguity of concepts. Problems are presented even by the choice of definition for a paradigm. Let us take here the Kuhnian community of researchers in a given discipline, who agree on the scope of the fundamental cognitive assumptions. But what would such a compromise involve? The common postulates include the nature of organizational reality (ontology), the way it is cognized (epistemology and methodology), the attitude towards values (axiology), and the criteria of scientific truths (correspondence, coherence, constructivist). The community of researchers of one paradigm shapes a feeling of identity, including through the founding of joint schools and institutional scientific undertakings (academic centres, publishing magazines, organizing conferences).

Vague criteria for distinguishing paradigms result in difficulties with deciding whether it is a basic division based on epistemological criteria or another, more detailed classification.

Irrespective of the difficulties described above, I propose conducting an analysis of the proposals for distinguishing paradigms in management science using the seven cognitive approaches mentioned earlier. In management science, there is deepening specialization, and within the field are subdisciplines of varying research methodology, subject, and approach, creating their own not always complementary discourses (Zsolnai, Junghagen, Tencati 2012). They are, to varying degrees, related to the sciences upon which management draws. An example of an incomplete and inseparable list of subdisciplines of management and quality sciences includes:

- Management methods and techniques;
- Business science;
- Organization theory;
- Entrepreneurship;
- Communication in the organization;
- Strategic management;
- Quality management;
- Production management;
- Public management;
- Human resources management;
- Leadership;
- Management of change in the organization;
- Innovativeness;
- Information and knowledge management;
- Marketing management;
- Financial management;
- Management accounting;
- International management.

Each of the fields of management indicated here has its own cognitive assumptions and would therefore constitute a separate paradigm. We can see here considerable fragmentation of paradigms that are suitable only for specialists of a given type of research problem. It is difficult to relate this to the broad definition of paradigm, which mentions the consensus among a larger community of researchers. Additionally, various cognitive assumptions can be pointed to within the subdisciplines themselves (such as the functionalist and interpretative paradigm of organizational culture). This classification of the subdisciplines of management, by definition generally accepted, generates numerous controversies in the academic community (for example, the distinguishing of public management). For these reasons, it is hard to place an equal sign between the subdisciplines and paradigms of management (Hitt 1997, pp. 1450–1455).

Numerous schools and trends have enriched the body of knowledge on management, but they have also complicated the issue. The chronological approach applies the criterion of the continuity of management school development. Taylor's 'scientific management', Fayol's 'administrative school', and Mayo's 'school of social relations' have different assumptions, but all are rooted in a common ontology, axiology, and concept of truth. The situation is similar for the division into trends (classical, neoclassical, psycho-social, and systemic). For this reason we must also draw a similar conclusion that a more general criterion for selecting paradigms is necessary.

G. Burrell and G. Morgan formulated definitions for the four fundamental paradigms in the social sciences. The researchers used the criteria of social orientation (regulation and change) and cognitive assumptions (objective and subjective). As a result of the intersection of these dimensions, we can distinguish four incommensurable paradigms: functionalistic, radical structuralism, interpretative, and radical humanism.

The first of these, which dominates in the social sciences, is called the 'functionalistic', 'neopositivist', 'positivist', 'systemic', or 'quantitative' paradigm (Holmwood 2005, pp. 87–109). For this paradigm, the natural sciences serve as a cognitive model. They combine the influences of the philosophy of neopositivism, the systemic trend, and functionalism originating in sociology and cultural anthropology. The legacy of the Vienna Circle included the following assumptions:

- Verificationism – enabling cognitive value to be determined thanks to empirical research, making it possible to answer the question what are the properties of the organization and how should it be effectively managed;
- The search for a dominant scientific method for assessing valuable knowledge;
- The division into dependent and independent variables, thanks to which cause-and-effect relationships can be built;
- The coherence and accumulation of knowledge – knowledge of the organization gathered thanks to research leads to progress;
- Striving for mathematical modelling that ensures a consistent picture of management science, expressed in the language of mathematics (operational research, simulations, forecasting);

- Quantifiability methodology – due to the necessity to carry out generalizations, quantitative methods are usually applied.

The neopositivist picture of management is not only the dominating paradigm but also a type of 'common sense' approach to our discourse. The next paradigm source is functionalism in sociology and cultural anthropology and its later critique. Characteristic for it is the assumption of maintaining a balance by the social whole in the process of exchange between elements of the social system (Kingsbury, Scanzoni 2009, pp. 195–221).

The actions of an organization's members serve this state. A 'function' is the contribution of individual actions to those of the whole. Thanks to functionalism, it is possible to distinguish complementary organizational functions in management that sustain the operation of the whole (for example, planning, organizing, monitoring, and motivating). Being in a state of functional balance, the system constitutes at the same time harmonious cooperation between subsystems. Functionalism directs us towards deterministic methodology in line with neopositivist thought, enabling understanding of the recurrence and patterns of social processes in the organization.

The third source of inspiration for the trend is the systems concept, situating the organization at the level of complex social systems (Outhwaite 2015, pp. 625–629). This concept features structural integration of subsystems within a greater whole as well as the emergence of system features at subsequent levels of complexity. We can say that the organization is a system striving to achieve balance with its surroundings in the processes of the flow of information and material resources; a system that can be controlled but to a limited degree. What links this concept with neopositivism? Certainly ambitions regarding the unity of science and the development of a scientific method based on a general systems theory. Meanwhile, the connection with functionalism concerns the concepts of system (functional) integration and homeostasis.

Neopositivist-functionalist-systems epistemology (abbreviation: NFS) is therefore characterized by the intention to verify the truth and an orientation towards creating integrated systems thanks to objective quantitative methods. This makes an analytical approach possible, within which generalizations of research results are made. We are dealing here with objective social processes of a cause-and-effect nature. The assumption is made of the axiological neutrality of science and the lack of interference of the researcher in building the most general social theories and mathematical modelling of the reality of the social sciences. Functionalists are often driven by the cognitive perspective of self-regulating social systems.

In management science, NFS has constituted the dominating cognitive formation throughout the entire development of this discourse. This may be due to the ambitions of the majority of theories to acquire universal knowledge and achieve a neopositivist scientific ideal. The theories created may be presented here as a sequence of causally related variables that can be subjected to mathematical formalization. In NFS, management features high generality, predictive power, and verificationism. The trends most deeply rooted in this approach are those originating in classical economics and the technical sciences that are related to the emergence of management science. There are also links with micro-economics, visible in the 'business sciences' thread. Qualitative methodology is used in many management subdisciplines (in management accounting or the management of logistics or information).

Critics of this trend refer to its mechanistic roots, which were superseded in physics by the theory of relativity and quantum mechanics. It is also criticized for depriving the social entity of autonomy and depicting a static image of the organization as well as for promoting the vision of a hyperrational individual. This is because in the enterprise we rarely have harmony but more often face a lack of balance, or disintegration and conflicts (Holmwood 2005, pp. 87–109). Searching for order may make it impossible to perceive the sense behind behaviours and interactions as well as explain the processes of exercising power, ownership, communicating, and building elements of organizational culture and reality (Wicks, Freeman 1998, pp. 123–140).

The emergence of the interpretive-symbolic paradigm occurred in opposition to functionalism (Barry 1996, pp. 411–438). It draws principally on the social and humanistic sciences – sociology, psychology, political science, and cultural anthropology. Among its principal assumptions we find:

- The cognitive function of language in shaping social reality;
- The links between cognitive activity and practice;
- Social constructivism;
- Use of qualitative methodology, originating mainly in the humanistic sciences.

Interpretative theories do not replicate the cause-and-effect schema used in neo-positivism but describe the interdependencies in complex social and organizational structures. It turns out that to create a scientific theory it is necessary for an engaged organizational member or also observer to discover meaning, rather than objectivism and axiological neutrality. Scientific constructs should show the intersubjective variations and interpretation of various organizational actors. These assumptions are the basis for many theories in management, above all those relating to organizational culture, human resources management, management processes, and managing change. Example concepts include *the management of meaning* by Morgan, Smircich, Czarniawska, and Magala; *sensemaking* by Weick; 'power networks' by Pfeffer and Salancik; and organizational identity by Albert and Whetten (Cronen, Chen, Pearce 1988, pp. 66–98; Lips-Wiersma, Morris 2009, pp. 491–511). The basis is the adoption of the constructivist and conventional nature of social and organizational reality. There is no objective organizational order; it is maintained and modified by groups or individuals operating around the organization and within it. Management processes are created in group processes of institutionalization, validation, and internalization and retain the character of collective consensus. Economic interests have the same power as political, social, or psychological influence. A person in the organization is value-oriented and engaged in research coupled with action, a seeker of meaning. Cognition is a symbolic act, tied up in language and culturally relativized. It is hard to talk of objective research results, only intersubjectively communicable ones. Notable may be the emphasis on the categories of everyday life, perception, interpretation, definition, the verification of usefulness, and action (the so-called epistemology of the everyday) (Suk-Young Chwe 2001, pp. 79–82).

This trend was criticized mainly on neopositivist-functionalist grounds, above all for the lack of generality of scientific theory. By giving only individual descriptions and conducting cultural studies within research into the organization, the issue of the development of the scientific field becomes uncertain.

The paradigm of radical structuralism, otherwise known as the critical trend (abbreviation: CMS – Critical Management Studies), assumes the existence of an objective social reality requiring fundamental transformation. Social truths are hidden within the micro- and macro-structures of power. How is the role of the social sciences perceived in this paradigm? It consists in finding hidden mechanisms of power, domination, and social inequality and in making changes – not only in the real world but also in social awareness. This is implemented by the researcher, who must first familiarize themselves with social mechanisms. This trend looks critically at reality and the achievements accumulated by the social sciences and uses qualitative research methods, mainly engaged methods (Cunliffe 2011, pp. 647–673; Hibbert et al. 2014, pp. 278–298).

The critical trend in management has its basis in philosophy, in which the organization is perceived as a source of power and domination (Fournier, Grey 2000, pp. 7–32; Spicer, Alvesson, Kärreman 2009, pp. 537–560; Pullen et al. 2017). This idea uses Bentham's metaphor of the panopticon and the class struggle of Marx (Kaghan 2005, pp. 353–375). In the 20th century, the oppressiveness of the organization was criticized by neo-Marxists, representatives of the Frankfurt School, poststructuralists, and postmodernists. Another point of reference is Jürgen Habermas's critical theory of communication. Foucault, the precursor of postmodernism, was of the opinion that power and domination are the engine of social action (e.g. the knowledge-power concept) and that obedience in society and in the organization is enforced through the use of surveillance and supervision. The mechanisms of inequality and power were also described by Bourdieu, who used the concept of 'symbolic violence'. Currently, this thinking is continued in the critical approach to the media and social communication as expressed by Hall and Deetz (1995) as well as in neo-Marxist feminism, which presents women as a group that is culturally dominated through manipulation of identity, false consciousness, and the above-mentioned symbolic violence (Oakley 2000).

Theories developed within the paradigm of radical structuralism (CMS) have several common assumptions. These are:

1 Research issues that include power, oppression, instrumentalism, and domination in management and in organizations.
2 Commitment to groups subject to oppression and the fight against the privileging of some groups at the expense of others. In management science discourse and managerial discourse, unequal social relations are camouflaged, rationalized, and ideologized. In CMS, the aim becomes the revealing of the injustices of disadvantage groups and their emancipation.
3 The axiological orientation of the researcher and the manager, and the entanglement of cognition and management in values. Language and culture cannot be neutral; they are a tool of domination. Change in the social order is possible thanks to engaged methods of cognition and action, leading to the abandonment of 'false consciousness'.
4 The dominating theory and practice of management rationalizes an unjust social order and preserves the reproduction of the ideology of managerialism. Therefore, the existing perception of management science was subject to radical criticism.

In management, representatives of CMS play on the one hand the role of whistleblower, while on the other hand they accelerate the processes of emancipation. This trend points to the pathologies of organization and management and strives to strengthen equality, justice, and human dignity in power relations. CMS is used in relation to the theory of organization, strategic management, human resources management, marketing, the management of information and organizational culture, and many other fields in the discourse on the organization (Saren, Svensson 2009).

This trend can be considered to be controversial due to its ideological assumptions. The maintaining of oppressive social structures by management is undoubtedly a one-sided way of perceiving. The *CMS* trend does however have scientific ambitions (the objectivism of neo-Marxism). Marxism proclaimed the 'scientificness' of its own discourse but never became anything other than an ideology.

In turn, the paradigm of radical humanism proposed by Burrell and Morgan would appear to be close to postmodernism, constituting an influential, although in the past two decades weakening, trend in contemporary humanities. At the same time it is the least homogeneous cognitive approach. Its inconsistency would seem to make calling it a paradigm risky. Common elements of this trend include mistrust of science, cognitive relativism, and subjectivism (Sim 2001, pp. 3–14). Representatives of poststructuralism, and then postmodernism, include authors such as Rorty, Baudrillard, Foucault, Derrida, Jameson, Lyotard, and also Bauman. Supporters of postmodernism question the possibility of arriving at objective truth. Such a radical position of cultural relativism with regard to science has its origins in the Edinburgh School of sociology of scientific knowledge programme, whose founders do not perceive science as a sphere of culture with a special status and treat the criteria of rationality, truth, and ways of experiencing reality as culturally and socially conditioned. Scientific theories are therefore a reflection of social ideologies. Postmodernists criticize the privileging of science in comparison to other fields of culture. From a historical perspective, Feyerabend condemned the imperialism of science, claiming that the 'apostles of science' suppress the representatives of other cultures, displacing their religions through the use of the 'religion of science' (Feyerabend 1975). The postmodernist trend illustrates the fall of the myth of progress, at the foundations of which lies uncritical striving for rationality, leading to the exploitation of reason against man. The most frequently used motives include:

- The lack of cognitive foundations and metanarrative;
- The crucial importance of discourse and language;
- The fragmentation of reality;
- Textualism (looking at reality using the metaphor of a text);
- Hyperreality (Alvesson, Deetz 2005).

The epistemological relativism of this trend leaves us with the problem of applying a scientific approach. The existence of a 'scientific theory' without the adoption of a correspondence or coherence theory of truth is meaningless. In moderate postmodernism, one can only talk about 'theorizing'.

In management, postmodernism occupies a marginal position. As in the case of other social sciences, it is simply a reaction to the fundamentalist ambitions expressed by neopositivists. Management owes to postmodernism the element of criticism, which does not lead to the deconstruction of its subject, but places cognition and social processes in the foreground (Clegg, Kornberger 2003). Postmodernism is a subjectivist, counter-intuitive, and relativist approach that is not shared by the majority of management researchers. In my view, it can be perceived as an intellectual provocation that draws attention to epistemological and ethical problems, and that is where its value lies. It can bring us closer to reflection on social and cultural relativism, subjectivism, the ethical context, and the responsibility and engagement of the researcher and employee.

Hatch connected the paradigms described above and highlighted by Burrell and Morgan from a historical perspective and proposed the following paradigms: classical, modernist, interpretative-symbolic, and postmodernist. At the cognitive foundations of the classical paradigm (whose representatives include Taylor, Weber, Fayol, and Barnard) lie functionalism and neopositivism (Melé, Cantón 2014, pp. 30–49). Modernism treats the organization in both functionalist and systemic categories. The interpretative-symbolic approach understands organization as the process of creating and discovering the organization's social reality. Postmodernism draws attention to the defragmentation and cultural and epistemological relativism present in textual and narrative approaches. The division of paradigms described above is particular to management science and also reaches back to the historical development of our discourse. However, it does not take into account the critical trend, which in the opinion of *CMS* researchers is a separate paradigm (Spicer, Alvesson, Kärreman 2009, pp. 537–560).

Johnson and Duberly proposed an epistemological typology for management science that draws on philosophy. The researchers identified five types of reflection found at the junction of the ontological and epistemological dimensions. In this typology, positivism, neopositivism, conventionalism, and pragmatism were added (they were not found in the Burrell and Morgan division) (Johnson, Duberley 2003, pp. 180–191). Objectivist ontology and epistemology are characterized by a positivist and neopositivist approach, constituting the equivalent of G. Burrell and G. Morgan's functionalism, as well as the classical and modernist schools, according to the classification by Hatch. Conventionalism, which like postmodernism makes use of subjectivist ontology and epistemology, leads to an increase in reflexivity thanks to the juxtaposition of difficult to compare metaphors and paradigms of organization and management. The critical trend and pragmatism are based on engaged cognition and the description of existing reality, that is to say they operate on the basis of objectivist ontology and subjectivist epistemology. Johnson and Duberly's concept is complementary to the vision of Burrell and Morgan with regard to the reflexivity of management science. In spite of this, the concept is relatively poorly recognized in management science as well as in the social sciences.

Bolman and Deal identified four 'cognitive frames' that enable a comprehensive understanding of the management process. These comprise the structural, human resource management, and political and symbolic approaches (Bolman, Deal 2003). The cognitive frames are an attempt to combine the dominant paradigm in the social sciences (structuralism, the symbolic approach) with a subdisciplinary approach (the political and human resources aspect). The authors illustrate their proposal with management problems that are visible thanks to the application of the above approach. The disadvantage of this concept is that it does not refer to the context of other social science disciplines and does not make use of the opportunities of various cognitive perspectives in management science. This is due to the fact that the approach lacks a critical trend, incremental strategy concepts, and a behavioural approach based on behavioural economics.

In his publication *Images of Organization*, Morgan proposes a different approach to the epistemology of management than in the case of the paradigms analysed jointly with Burrell. The basis is a specific metaphor for the organization which determines the researcher's actions in the organization (Morgan 1998). Eight metaphorical images were to be the basis for a pluralistic understanding of the organization. The organizing metaphor recognized by researchers and managers is a conceptual and pragmatic frame for reflection and action. The use of mechanistic, cultural, cognitivist, organic, and also psychodynamic metaphors reveals the stereotypes and types of discourse functioning in management theory and practice. However, Morgan does not consider organization metaphors to be management paradigms. Paradigms are of a more general nature and should be taken into consideration in the collective achievements of a given science.

The cognitive perspectives in management science described above do not constitute all proposals. Remenyi, Williams, Money, and Swartz proposed two complementary research perspectives: positivism and phenomenology (Remenyi et al. 2005, pp. 32–37). Jackson, working on the basis of systemic thinking, described the elementary cognitive assumptions of management using 12 ways of understanding the organizational system (Jackson 2003). The selection of management paradigm typologies is therefore burdened with similar ambiguity to the previously mentioned problems of the theory or definition of organization and management.

The emergence of paradigms turned out to be crucial for the formulation of theory and the selection of research methods in management. A paradigm would appear to a large degree to determine the approach not only to theory or methodology but also to research issues and axiological orientation (Table 3.1).

Management science theories use various paradigms, as can be seen in their components, results, and key threads as well as in the researcher's attitude and the selection of methodology. Assessment of the cognitive value of a given management theory is possible only after prior identification of the paradigm that became the point of reference. Methodological justification is not necessary if the dominating paradigm is selected, as it constitutes a way of perceiving and researching organizational reality that has been verified and scientifically accepted. However, using alternative paradigms in constructing a cognitive theory requires broader methodological justification.

The use of Burrell and Morgan's paradigm concepts in management science is not without consequences. However, it is an approach that can be applied in management, psychology, sociology, and cultural anthropology. The essence of this approach is placing emphasis on interdisciplinary threads, but its generality is also a limitation, obscuring the specificity of a given discipline.

The canon of neopositivism (also known as logical empiricism) was created at the beginning of the 20th century by a group of philosophers centred around the Vienna Circle (Hodgson 2007, pp. 96–114). Its echo in management is not only the Taylorist and Fayolian trend but also the canon of scientific method modelled on the natural sciences. Neopositivist ideals of a general theory of science did not meet with success; however, the cognitive problems of logical empiricism had an indirect impact on many disciplines. Researchers consciously or unconsciously reached for neopositivist criteria of valuable knowledge, and

Table 3.1 Structure of scientific theory and management paradigms

Criterion	*Paradigm*			
	functional-systemic	*interpretative-symbolic*	*critical*	*postmodernism*
Theory components	Theorems, definitions Hypotheses Statements of fact Variables Causal relationships	Theoretical constructs Interpretations Interdependencies Descriptions and studies	Theoretical constructs Statements of fact Actors and groups Structures of power and interests	Narrations Discourses Glosses Theoretical constructs
Theory objectivism	Objectivism	Intersubjectivism	Intersubjectivism	Subjectivism
Theory verification	Verificationism or falsificationism	Interpretivism and constructivism	Interpretivism and also weak verificationism	Constructivism
Result of theorizing	Sequential relationships of cause-and-effect variables	Interpretation of organizational actors immersed in networks of meaning	Exposing accounts of hidden relationships of power and oppression, leading to action	Autopoietic discourses leading to ethical reflection
Role in management	Dominating	Increasing	Increasing	Marginal
Dominating methodology	Quantitative	Qualitative	Qualitative	None or qualitative
Most important theoretical threads	Strategy Structure Management functions Organization theory	Language Organizational culture Organizational behaviours	The person in the organization Power Oppression manipulation Managerialism ideology Denaturalization of management	Organizational textualism – rhetoric, poetics, archetypes, metaphors, moral paradoxes Problems of managerialism
Attitude to values	Axiological neutrality	Moderate axiological neutrality	Engagement in valuing	Engagement in valuing

Source: Own elaboration.

the achievements of logical empiricism have been developed among others by representatives of realism.

Exclusion of metaphysics and its concepts from the field of science:

1 Development of rules for arriving at the truth, that is a 'scientific method';
2 The pursuit of verifiable scientific knowledge;
3 The search for a logical, physicalistic language that can be used for the objective description of reality;
4 The foundation of all sciences on the model of empiricism from the natural sciences;
5 The mathematical formalization of scientific theories and laws in the natural and social sciences.

To create a science, it was necessary to reject metaphysics, treated as a field without subject matter and unknowable from a scientific point of view. Only observational statements could be scientific, while at the same time, the tautological nature of true judgements of logic and mathematics was recognized. This was related to the postulate to rely on empirical data, leading to logical and mathematical reductions and generalizations. Sciences created on the basis of these assumptions should be verifiable and lead to certain knowledge. Referring critically to the postulate of the certainty of knowledge, Popper modified the category of verifiability, presenting the criterion of falsifiability: 'The rules of the empirical method should be designed in such a way that they not protect any scientific statement from falsification'. Hypotheses that we consider falsifiable fulfil the criterion of scientific discourse.

The model for the neopositivist approach in the social sciences were the natural sciences. A trace of this concept in management science is the approach to the organization as to an object that can be understood using a methodology akin to that of the natural sciences. Taylor, one of the 'founding fathers', expounded an open approach to radical neopositivist criteria of science in relation to management. He called for the creation of science:

- That is experimental, examining the impact of variables on the social situation;
- Using universal and objective theories and methods (that is modelled on the natural sciences);
- That is mathematicized and formalized, capturing management processes in the form of formulae, models, and mathematical functions;
- That is reductionist, in which it is possible to examine the causal impact of variables on the management process;
- That is verifiable, fulfilling the criteria of deterministic causal explanation and prediction.

Meanwhile, F.W. Taylor noted the pragmatism of management, manifesting itself in the need to apply theories in organizational practice. This engineering approach differs from the neopositivist ideal of science proposed by the representatives of the Vienna Circle. Despite criticism, the neopositivist image of management continues to function in the minds of management researchers, at times liberating them from the need to investigate cognitive foundations. However, researchers cannot free themselves of the cognitive context and focus exclusively on analytical work. Management without cognitive bases (which the natural sciences do possess) can be compared to a building without foundations.

Verificationism was subject to criticism by the critical rationalist trend. The first of these researchers underlined the impossibility of fully verifying scientific theorems due to the use of incomplete induction. However, he proposed the concept of falsificationism, according to which it is not possible to prove that a given scientific theorem is true, but that it can at least be rejected, that is falsified. Theorems and scientific theories are falsifiable in nature, that is they are potentially refutable, but one cannot merely refute pseudosciences (Popper used this term for not only astrology but also, for example, psychoanalysis). The situation is similar for many management concepts. It is not possible to empirically refute systemic organization models (e.g. by Leavitt or Morgan) or the concept of network organization. Reference to empirics is often merely for appearances, and the complexity of realities allows for many conflicting interpretations of observed situations. Although verificationism dominates in thinking, management does not meet the criteria of even the least rigorous falsificationism. Many researchers try at all costs to hold on to these ideas, even though they no longer dominate in contemporary philosophy of science. It is better to follow other criteria of valuable knowledge in management, other concepts useful in the practice of our discourse.

In spite of everything, the category of verifiability plays an important role in management science. Within the research procedure, hypotheses are posed and then require empirical verification. Methodological rigour is of key importance as it enables the research process to be monitored both with criticism and also with trust in the research results. With regard to verification, researchers make use of criteria for accepting or rejecting hypotheses. Instead of such criteria, scientific works make increasing use of theses that are not subject to verification or research questions posed in order to deepen knowledge. Management science sanctions such relaxation of procedures; however, the scientific ideal still remains the following cognitive process: hypothesis, verification, and theory.

Is the subject of management science, that is organizations, specific or metaphysical? According to orthodox neopositivist criteria, we have a metaphysical subject of research, and organizations and management processes are hard to describe. However, neither the lack of a clear definition nor metaphysicality implies a lack of scientificity in management. Let us draw attention to the social function of the discourse, rejecting neopositivist criteria. Management is a science, created by the scientific community, with scientific institutions, and guided by internal rules of discipline. The products of management created by academia and the consulting community constitute scientific knowledge.

The majority of management researchers concentrate on development in their discourse. The accumulation of knowledge and the construction of a management monolith may remind us of the biblical tower of Babel. The bricklayers use different concepts and a different language, which can lead to chaos. It is difficult to agree on one position with regard to the organization among so many subdisciplines. It is treated one way by 'scientific management' and another by the school of 'social relations'. We could even say that there is a 'jungle of theories', which can confuse many researchers. For this reason, in management there is no accumulation of knowledge in its straightforward meaning as there is no single paradigm and even a lack of criteria for comparing the values of various concepts. There is an accumulation of information, but it is hard to say whether it constitutes valuable knowledge or just informational noise. The creation of theories in management is far from the generalizations in the natural sciences and is closer to the understanding of the humanities.

The next important problem in management is the issue of searching for a 'scientific method'. Which of the proposed approaches to the method can be found in management science? The non-existence of rules governing the value of knowledge could tempt us to adopt Feyerband's (1993) 'anything goes' position. This is a type of neopragmatism, which assumes that every methodological solution is acceptable if it enables a creative approach to an organizational problem. However, experts stress the value of quantifiable methods, findings, and results, that is traces of the 'scientific method' of the natural sciences. This may be the origin of the preference for statistically representative methods as well as the belief that only research based on statistical and random sampling allows for generalizations. Meanwhile, researchers do at times ignore methodological imperfections, for example, the lack of random sampling or too low numbers. The most popular research technique in management continues to be the survey, and qualitative methods are often discredited (such as the anthropology of the organization, case study comparative analysis, in-depth interviews, and discourse analysis). Many researchers are simply not accustomed to the use of qualitative methods in the social sciences. In researching management issues, seldom is use made of ethnomethodology, qualitative text analysis, projective psychological methods, grounded theory, *action research,* or the sociology of intervention. Here, it is important to emphasize the value of applying varied research methods in management, including qualitative methods. No one single method has been found that would allow other methodological propositions to be rejected. For this reason, it is worth reaching for methodological triangulation in order to solve not only the problems of the organization but also the problems of scientific management (Love, Holt, Li 2002).

This does not mean that we have no criteria at our disposal for assessing the value of knowledge but that these criteria depend on the management paradigm.

Management science is modal and dependent both on the cognitive context and its application. According to the 'uncertainty principle' metaphor originating in physics and developed by Heisenberg or the Hawthorne effect, the researcher is usually aware that in the course of researching reality, they are also changing it. There is no cognitive certainty; however, we can say that management is developing, concepts are changing, and new schools are being formed. In my opinion, social and pragmatic criteria play a key role in such development, with the development of the discipline driven in a given environment thanks to specialists and managers. The most important development criteria include:

- The simplicity and aesthetics of the theoretical structure;
- The originality of the concept and its practical implications;
- Consistency with existing concepts (cohesion), which unfortunately often leads to a lack of originality;
- The economic effectiveness and efficiency of the solutions applied in the organization.

Various groups play differing roles in the evaluation of the developed concepts. Scientists usually focus on the criterion of consistency due to their conservative views and broad knowledge of other concepts. For organization advisors and managers, economic effectiveness seems to be more important, as well as the aesthetics of the concept and its originality. Consulting firms often contribute to the popularization of a given concept as a method for generating profits thanks to marketing actions that arouse demand for their services. Meanwhile, in seeking competitive solutions, managers may lean more towards aesthetic and seemingly universal management concepts.

The problem of reaching for cause-and-effect schema and the resulting division into dependent and independent variables is a classical dilemma of scientific methodology. The ideal is research into the influence of individual variables, but the experimental method is of limited application in the social sciences. Organizational variables are interdependent, and changes in one area lead to changes in others. The organization should therefore be viewed from a holistic perspective, and the conventional division of variables should be adopted as the agreed and approximate research approach.

This is recognized by selected researchers of the systems, social and interpretative approach, the chaos concept, the fractal organization, the cultural trend, and the learning organization. However, some researchers continue to insist on the cause-and-effect approach, obtaining very simple interpretations. The link between management and neopositivist theories allows two important conclusions to be drawn. Firstly, no discipline in the social sciences can meet the orthodox criteria of the scientificity of neopositivism, the more so management. Secondly, logical empiricism, which was based solely on natural science and recognized monism in science (the cognitive uniformity of science and the assumption that differences in the subject of research do not constitute a barrier in the use of the same methods and generalizations), was adopted in management only in a highly simplified form. However, the social sciences differ significantly from the natural sciences, which is why neopositivist concepts are misplaced in management. This is explained by the dualism of science, according to which universal laws are not formulated in the social sciences. At this stage of development, I am in favour of differentiating between scientific rules in the natural sciences and in the social sciences. Contemporary management is not made up of general laws and theories, only generalizations, medium-range theories and microtheories, and metaphors and analogies. There are also local theories (microtheories), as in sociology, which do not constitute models or systems but only solutions and their generalizations in given social conditions. In my view, management investigates such complex social dependencies that it is difficult to speak of higher levels of generalization. Emphasis should be placed on generalizations of a shorter range, not on the whole system. Abstractions in management are hermetic organizational models that are of little use and impractical, the opposite of medium-range generalizations and the pragmatic solutions proposed in various subdisciplines, which are expressed in the organization's activity and can be corroborated with experience (here I purposefully do not use the term verifiable).

It is difficult to speak at all of neopositivism in contemporary science. Certain elements can be found in the critical rationalism propagated by Albert and Popper, but the division applied within this into metaphysics and empirical knowledge is no longer valid. However, the mythology of scientism remained in management, visible in the numerous references to logical empiricism, in the preference for quantitative methods, and in the forcing of social processes into mathematical models. The almost ritual procedure of posing hypotheses and subjecting them to verification in research studies at times becomes a kind of mythology cultivated by the academic community in mainstream management. Of course, there are good reasons for such procedures, but they should not be granted the status of being the only correct procedures. Alongside the posing of hypotheses there is the possibility to pose questions and make inquiries, reflected in the dualism of the English term *research-inquiry*. The methodology of the natural and social sciences differs. In management, experiments are seldom used, with observational and interrogative methods applied instead. The preference for quantitative over qualitative methods, which differentiates management from, for example, sociology, cultural anthropology, linguistics, and political science, may stem from the above-mentioned bending of methods to suit criteria originating in the natural sciences.

Management is close to the engineering approach (the scientific management trend), the social approach (the school of social relations), the cultural approach oriented towards power, the political approach, and others. Currently, the way the subject of research is viewed is changing. What remains permanent are only the institutional aspects (scientists, research, and academic centres) and practical aspects (organizations, managers, and employees). Management therefore constitutes a certain self-reflection of society of practical importance. However, full reflection requires critical analysis of the subject of research and also a return to cognitive basics.

Neopositivism views the role of the researcher differently, it strives for objectivism and non-interference, while in the social sciences interference is necessary, and researching the organization usually requires a change in the subject under study (the Hawthorne effect). The researcher cognizes in a process of incessant changes, which is why precise and permanent measurement is not possible. Research is therefore valuable when it can be related to practice. Echoes of the myth of researcher objectivity can still be heard in management, but in fact the researcher's value system affects the interpretations they make. In management, the essence of research is always interwoven with its social context.

To sum up, the neopositivist canon of valuable knowledge, which includes generality, certainty, precision, informativeness, and simplicity, cannot be related directly to the social sciences. Only the apparent scientific restrictiveness of neopositivism perpetuates the importance of conventional methods, coherent with previous methods. The lack of agreement for the use of qualitative methods limits the development of management. However, it should be noted that on the plus side for logical empiricism is its cognitive optimism and belief in progress, which, along with precision, rigour, and regularity in science, belong to positive approaches. Management also makes use of neopositivism as part of attempts to create new paradigms like neo-evolutionism or representative formalism.

Evolutionism can help in interpreting many collective behaviours that are the basis of organization and management. In the social sciences, there are two contradictory visions of the individual. The first, originating in the technical and exact sciences, and characteristic for economics, recognizes the rationality of individuals' decisions (*homo oeconomicus*). H. Simon corrected economic thought and showed that we have limited rationality due to a lack of access to complete information. In the epistemological sense, this is related to a reductionist and individualistic position. Economic behaviours can be assessed as the actions of individuals who are rational but do not have access to full information. In the second vision of the individual, found in the humanistic sciences (in sociology and anthropology), emotions and irrational actions dominate in people's behaviours (*homo sociologicus*). At the epistemological level, this represents an antireductionist and collectivist position, and the description of the actions of individuals is formed on the basis of the functioning of social groups and cultures (Kirchgässner 2008). This dichotomy, which is over 100 years old, is beginning to become irrelevant. Currently, empirical research conducted as part of *neuroscience*, cognitive science, and evolutionary psychology draws a new picture of 'human nature'. This would appear to be closer to the concept of *homo sociologicus*. Human destiny is mainly reproduction and genetic recombination, with survival and development of the individual only coming later. The human brain is tasked with increasing the chances of reproduction and survival of the human race. Our decision-making processes are characterized by emotionality. False memory, illusions of identity, intentionality, and other cognitive features limit – from the point of view of rationality – our perception, reasoning, and decision-making.

The first consequence of the presence of the evolutionist paradigm in the social sciences is the development of sociobiology and evolutionary psychology. What organizational problems have evolutionary foundations? These may include, for example:

- Group communication;
- Group and organizational ties;
- Learning in organizations;
- Leadership in the organization and the natural source of the power structure;
- Taking risk;
- The biological roots of organizing;
- Sexual behaviour;
- Competition, conflict, and the struggle for domination;
- Cultural conditions for organizations and societies.

Although at first glance evolutionary research does not relate to problems of the organization, its interpretations do however have an impact on human behavioural science. In management processes, for example, both communication and the struggle for domination become apparent. Accepting the assumption that men and women have different cognitive and emotional apparatus may help to explain the differences between 'male' and 'female' management styles. An over-rationalized vision of human nature (close to *homo oeconomicus*) appears in theories of recruitment, motivation, and development used in human resources management. Decision-making processes are often beyond the control of consciousness, which may contribute to a revision of the theory of personnel management (Colarelli 2003). Organizational behaviours and marketing should take into account evolutionary motives for human actions, relating, for example, to the behaviour value system that serves survival or the selection of partners. Allowing for evolutionary interpretations leads to a better understanding of how money works, e.g. risk factors, playing the stock market, the phenomena of saving and extravagance, etc. Strategic management can make use of knowledge originating in Darwinism. Planning, awareness of time, and the propensity to take risks are more easily explained using the biological foundations of the human cognitive and emotional apparatus. Thanks to evolutionism, management has a chance of understanding 'human nature', while without it there are difficulties in explaining the processes of leadership and exercising power, communication, conflict and cooperation, and also relationships and the differences between the sexes. A new paradigm – neo-evolutionism – has at its disposal research and theory which together make up a coherent picture of the individual in the environment.

'Human nature', whose roots are found in the history of the human race and other species, appears in many areas of management (in personnel management, organizational sociology, marketing theory, etc.). Issues that constitute a subject of research for evolutionists, and which are a focus of interest in management, are:

- The creation of organizational processes, social structures, and power structures – based on social ties;
- The basics of communication and language and their impact on the issue of identification with the group;
- Struggle and conflict within the group and between individuals;
- Competition, risk-taking, leadership, and domination;
- Sexual behaviour, the differences between the sexes and their effect on social and organizational ties (Haselton, Buss 2004).

An evolutionary-rooted theory of the organization should take into account the needs and shape of the human cognitive and emotional apparatus. This involves the need to search for a 'second meaning' in the motives behind actions, that is strengthening the position of the individual and physical or symbolic reproduction. People's needs, fears, imagination, and emotions are rooted in millions of years of social experiences.

In seeking evolutionary inspiration for the development of organizational structures, we must refer to the concept of power and hierarchy. A search can be made for the paths of development of organizational processes and the crystallization of authority. The influence of evolutionary laws on formalized structures seems difficult to name at present. But power and hierarchy are themselves rooted in the human mind and have biological foundations.

Organizational strategy can be related to the concept of planning and games (De Dreu, Gross 2019). The development of cognitive abilities brought with it the possibility to plan the future and the ability to participate in multivarious games that allow the right solutions to be chosen. The strategies selected by leaders bring consequences for the collectivity, and the mechanisms of taking decisions are not an entirely conscious process. One of these is making decisions based on intuition. According to Damasio, intuitive decisions can manifest themselves somatically and emotionally, for example, we may experience stomach cramp when we have a fear of excessive risk. Researchers suggest that we take many decisions unconsciously, in an instant, while our conscious interpretation is merely a rationalization conducted at a later stage (Gladwell 2005). In leadership processes there is also a struggle for domination in the group as well as attempts to build a coalition and communicate. Constructing psychological and social profiles for leaders and preparing a description of their cooperation with the group constitute a considerable challenge (Lawrence, Pirson 2015, pp. 383–394). The examples cited above are from different subdisciplines and relate to various issues. Neo-evolutionism can provide an interpretative framework that makes it possible to deepen our hitherto understanding of people and organizations.

How does this thinking relate to other paradigms? The closest paradigm would seem to be NFS, which assumes the objectivity of cognition, rationality, and verificationism and uses research methods based on the natural sciences. The vision of the institution and human nature and the adaptive function of human behaviours have a great deal in common with neo-evolutionism. However, functionalism overestimates the role of culture in forming the social world, at the cost of genetic conditions. There is also no explanation regarding the essence of reproduction, which is an important criterion due to the 'egoism of genes'.

Neo-evolutionism differs significantly – both on an epistemological and on a methodological level – from the interpretative-symbolic paradigm, in which of key importance are cognitive subjectivity, dualism, and the basing of methods on hermeneutics and phenomenology. The differences are quite obvious, but can any similarities be found? In interpretivism, the individual is not *homo oeconomicus*, as in the NFS paradigm, but an individual bound up in meanings of which they are the author and driven by internally inconsistent emotional and intellectual motivation. Neo-evolutionism moves away from perceiving the individual as a being with an exclusively rational mind, emphasizing that they are also subject to instincts related to reproduction, survival, social life, etc. However, evolution as well as the redundancy of the human brain (exaptation) led to the existence of higher needs. Various needs and motivations, both conscious and unconscious, co-exist in the human mind. When describing human behaviour, one cannot stop at the rational sphere and not take into account cognitive illusions and emotions.

Neo-evolutionism is the opposite of radical structuralism, in which the vision of an entity involved in the process of change and its attitude towards emancipatory change in and negation of the epistemology of neopositivism stand in opposition to neoevolutionism. This, meanwhile, does not recognize the 'critical theory' as any more than an ideology. The only common feature is the vision of the individual and society as devoid of illusions. The critical trend attributes egoistic categories to the social world. Here, the individual desires power, ownership wants to meet their needs and control resources, and society is an extension of these desires. Social institutions are oppressive in nature and maintain an unjust order. This 'state of order' can be demolished by revolutionary activity involving wronged social groups. Neo-evolutionism also notes the egoistic efforts of individuals, who idealize their arguments and rationalize their actions, including nepotism. Here, altruism is far from selflessness, as in helping our kin we take into account our common genes, while thanks to cooperation with strangers we have a greater chance of survival. Fortunately, neither evolutionism nor the critical trend opts for full egoistic determinism. Genetic 'programming' is not behavioural automation and can only relate to certain tendencies that can be overcome by the individual. The creation of both paradigms seems to be proof of the superiority of humans over biological mechanisms.

Neo-evolutionism and radical humanism (sometimes identified with post-modernism) are entirely different. Postmodernism can be defined as relativistic and subjective, demonstrating scepticism towards science. Meanwhile, neo-evolutionism is objective and looks for generalizations and universalism and is thus characterized by trust in science.

4 The Challenges of Current Paradigms in Management Science

In recent decades, management science has seen the birth of many concepts rooted in the humanities, which we can place in an interpretative perspective (Ridder, Hoon 2009, pp. 93–106). It was begun by symbolic interactionism in sociology and cultural anthropology, the symptoms of which we can see in the historical and political sciences, philosophy, and linguistics (Wright, Losekoot 2012, pp. 416–422). This trend is rarely used in organizational discourse, but many of its assumptions have been adapted in management science, which is why it is worth taking a moment here for reflection. The interpretative-symbolic paradigm is to a large degree identified with qualitative research methodology in the subject literature (Åsvoll 2014, pp. 289–307). However, it would seem that qualitative research is also used through the critical paradigm, as well as in mixed quantitative-qualitative research in functionalism.

In management, there are currently the following epistemological assumptions, realized with the aid of qualitative methodology: social constructivism, the cognitive role of language, the intertwining of cognitive activity in practice, and social consensus. In the epistemological sense, we are dealing with an entity that is reflexive, involved in relationships, and cognizing reality. In constructivism, reality is created socially. Weick (in the process of organizing), as well as Berger and Luckmann (in social processes), agreed that reality is created by social actors. The majority of the social and organizational world does not objectively exist, neither interpersonal ties, nor power, nor communication; everything is intersubjective and is created *implicite* and *explicite* in the processes of negotiating meanings, both group and individual. The reality of the organization also has material foundations, which ontologically are objective assets, for example, machines or raw materials. In the organization, a feedback loop occurs in objective reality, which is subjected to the process of interpretation and given meaning. Social conventions form around it and have an influence on it.

The described trend adopted moderate social constructivism (in contrast to radical postmodernist options). Man is here the creator of the world, giving it sense thanks to interpretation. Interpretative reasoning draws attention to the tension between the individual's exploration and creation of the world in the

DOI: 10.4324/9781003530947-6

process of cognition. The entity is both the explorer and the creator. Reality is not only a social or linguistic construct as cultural components are also important.

Researchers of social constructivism in this orientation analyse the organization on the basis of social processes related to conferring and interpreting meanings. In management, examples of this thinking include the concepts: the management of meanings (most important authors: Magala, Czarniawska, Morgan, Smircich), identity and organizational culture (Smircich, Hatch), dominant strategy logic and organizational subcultures (Van Maanen, Barley) (Ravasi, Schultz 2006, pp. 433–458).

In many social trends it has been accepted that language, in its cultural understanding, is the cognitive basis for understanding the world. Concepts in organization and management have multiple meanings and are fluid. Terms that make up the sphere of organizing (such as identity, leadership, organizational structure, culture, power, and strategy) do not have a single designation and can be defined in different ways.

This variability in social meanings is linked to constructivist reasoning. The way of naming creates a specific and non-uniform discourse of many trends. The social nature and linguistic character of cognition results in the ambiguity of management, in which it is not possible to propose universal theories or create a single discourse. Such desires are a kind of utopia associated with the Lyotardian 'metanarratives' occurring in radical epistemological fundamentalism. How does this approach differ from postmodernism? Here, cognition and changes to reality do actually occur, rather than mere participation in linguistic games. Cognizing and thinking about management processes form a hermeneutic circle (Boell, Cecez-Kecmanovic 2010, pp. 129–144). Language does not have to be an ideal reflection of reality; it creates it (the constructivist and pragmatic approach) and sets the boundaries of knowledge and sense. In management we have intersubjective cognitive constructs, such as structure, culture, and strategy, and also the enterprise and its surroundings.

This trend discusses the dependencies between research and the modification of the researched reality. Management has always drawn upon the engineering approach, in which the design and implementation of optimalization processes and their monitoring were crucial. Simple, deterministic tools of change were replaced with refined tools requiring reflection. The aim remains similar, that is to increase the effectiveness and efficiency of management and the development of the organization. Inspired by neopragmatism, management strives rather to transform the world and not simply describe it.

The researcher is not an objective observer but is involved – in commencing research they decide to engender change in the organization. Mayo noted that the researcher has an influence on the people and situations under study (the Hawthorne effect). In management, it is therefore difficult to speak of a clear division into the subject and object of research.

Colloquial explanation is not worse than scientific explanation. Researchers of management use everyday language or the much more closed language of theory. Interpreters in management face the challenge of interpreting both languages – refined terminology and the colloquial discourse of new 'management gurus'.

Such thinking is typical, for example, for change management, human resources management, strategic management, organizational learning, and understanding of organizational culture and identity. Order in an organization is a subjective phenomenon that is maintained and reconstructed by members of the organization. Management processes occur as a result of group institutionalization, validation, and internalization, which constitute collective consensus. Economic interests have a similar scope of influence as social, psychological, and political interests. Within organizational order, social structures emerge that are the subject of conventions. Of such a nature are, for example, charismatic leadership, authority, organizational identity, informal groups or subcultures, organizational strategy, and hierarchy, which make up social consensus. This is maintained by participants in the life of the organization. Such conventions are of varying strength and duration. Social conventions have their legal basis. Trust in their duration and the involvement of members of the organization in the game being played are deciding factors in the continuity of the organization.

The process of negotiating meanings is not purely rational. For members of the organization, reality is something obvious, but in actual fact a social game is constantly in progress on an unconscious level. Since the act of cognition has become entangled in language and culture, it is thus a symbolic activity (Schnackenberg et al. 2019, pp. 375–413). Symbolic behaviours are the carrier and expression of organizational roles. The symbols of position, function, and status in the organization are symptoms of power, while organizational culture is a symbolic system. Structural and strategic processes are also based on symbolic systems, the consequences of which are the entanglement of management in context, both semantic and linguistic.

Researchers of organizational culture and identity underline the role of management as a symbolic activity. According to Hatch, artefacts, values, and symbols are created in culture through interpretation. With increasing frequency, management is addressing problems stemming from the analysis of symbolic culture, for example, the anthropology of everyday life and organizational identity (Hatch, Schultz 2004).

Such a division of methodologies can be seen in cultural research in sociology, linguistics, and cultural anthropology and to a lesser degree in management, particularly in Poland. How can it be applied in research, especially research into organizational culture? As early as the 1950s, the linguist Pike emphasized the variation in research methods on social behaviours. He analysed individuals' linguistic behaviours but saw the possibility for using this dichotomy in research on social behaviours. These concepts are abbreviations created from the terms *phonemic* and *phonetic*. This methodological division was accepted in ethnology and cultural anthropology but was also shown to be of assistance in culture research in other disciplines (psychology, psychiatry, medicine, sociology, and

Table 4.1 The methodologies of *emic* and *etic* in cultural research

Methodology	Emic	Etic
Epistemological background	The interpretative-symbolic paradigm Hermeneutics Phenomenology	Axiological neutrality and objectivism of the neopositivist paradigm
Characteristics	Particular research categories are embedded in social reality The subject of discourse are everyday contextual concepts rooted in culture	Reality exists objectively, and the role of the research process is to reflect it thanks to scientific method Universal frames of reference originate from outside culture. Efforts are made to achieve objectivism and generalizations
Role of the researcher	They understand culture and approach it analytically An *Insider*, taking part	An *Outsider*, external and not involved An observer maintaining their distance
Research methods	Cultural studies Interviews Participant observations Other qualitative and anthropological methods	Surveys Statistics Other quantitative methods used in empirical sciences
Examples	A. Tourraine's sociology of intervention A. Strauss's grounded theory C. Geertz's 'dense description'	Cultural research involving an external observer

Source: Own elaboration.

archaeology) as well as sporadically in management. This distinction is shown in Table 4.1.

1 Qualitative methodology of the interpretative-symbolic paradigm;

Management is increasingly reaching for methods from this trend, and there is a transfer of methods from linguistics, sociology, cultural anthropology, and social psychology (Bluhm et al. 2011, pp. 1866–1891). The most popular research method are:

- Grounded theory;
- Participant research;
- In-depth case studies;
- Ethnomethodology;
- Metaphorical methods;
- Organizational anthropology;
- Visual anthropology;
- Sociology of intervention;
- Humanistic psychology methods.

The above methods are examples of qualitative research and field studies. An engaged researcher attempts to understand the organization and its members in the process of action, using everyday categories. The method of learning is also a method of improvement. An important role is played by culture, language, and the axiological element. Of course, this method has also been the subject of criticism, mainly due to the fact that it is not objective, and it is difficult to compare the research results or confirm their reliability. It is not possible to investigate mass phenomena in this way, and an engaged researcher may raise doubts of an ethical nature.

The epistemological assumptions of the interpretative trend found their place in many management concepts. In addition to those mentioned above, it is worth mentioning such examples as the dramaturgical perspective, the locating and transfer of meanings, creating cognitive maps, organizational learning, and life history methodology. The application of this approach enables a functional take on the management process, which can be viewed through the lens of the formation of organizational culture, the creation and interpreting of strategy, and the structurization of the enterprise.

The cognitive perspective is found in the interpretative-symbolic paradigm; here the organization constitutes a social domain of a clash of meanings and the interests of actors and social groups. Managers shape the conditions of the organizational game, in which various groups participate, that is employees, clients, and partners. As part of the organizational game, there is an investment of financial, social, and cultural capital, with an expected return on this investment. In the interpretative-symbolic sense, the economic game is closer to Wittgenstein's 'language game' than the model of the ideal *homo oeconomicus*. Engagement in the 'game' is spontaneous, and investments are made intuitively. Organization members, that is the players, share a collective identity. Organizations constitute a whole from an economic and legal perspective and also a psychological and social perspective and function as a dynamic system between openness to the surroundings and closure allowing for the preservation of identity (Kirchner 2013, pp. 35–54).

The organization can be described from the point of view of:

- The processes of foreseeing and designing changes, also in the surroundings;
- Cultural values, patterns, and norms (that is organizational cultures and identity);
- The processes of power and communication manifesting themselves in the structure.

It is worth supplementing the interpretative vision of the organization with inspirations originating in the trend that adopted the name cognitive. Cognition, a derivative of reality, is conditioned by the cognitive apparatus of individuals and groups (mind and culture). The developing cognitive perspective in management can be described using the following assumptions:

1 The organization is an intersubjective entity; thus in researching it to discover meanings, the participant perspective should be adopted rather than the objectivist and generalizing methods used in the natural sciences (the method applied here is, for example, cognitive cartography).
2 The organization exists at the level of individual and collective (intersubjective) meanings, which brings the cognitive perspective closer to the non-functionalist concept of organizational culture.
3 The organization is both a symbolic and material product of individuals and groups. It can be understood thanks to such cognitive processes as perception, the creation of meanings, and interpretation. It constitutes not only the subject of the management process but also its result. Cognitive processes are our cultural and biological equipment. Reality is perceived through filters (language, gender, the categories of time and space, etc.), which manifest themselves in cognitive patterns. They are the answer to the desire to organize reality and can take the form of cognitive structures or cognitive products, as well as stereotypes. Thanks to them, we interpret the world of the organization by referring to our own imagination.
4 We transfer ideas from our experiences to the area of management through metaphors. Everyday experiences are the primary categories of giving meaning and understanding, wherein here we mean everyday experiences for organization members, and theoretical constructs for organization researchers.

This cognitive concept of management reaches for the interpretative paradigm, as it captures organizational activity in terms of intersubjective meanings. Other cognitive theories are also related to the interpretative trend, some of which have a neopositivist perspective. The objective picture is a myth; what counts are motivation, interests, and stereotypes. It is not possible to understand objective reality in the process of communication, we can only create 'cognitive bridges' that are nothing more than social consensus.

Although P. Cossett's cognitive approach is in line with the interpretative trend, it is worth pointing out the differences. In the cognitive approach, the cognitive apparatus is created from a combination of an individual's biological equipment and a cultural vision of cognitive patterns, while the interpretative trend is more related to culturalism. The use of cognitive patterns rather than language games or social constructs constitutes a new perspective. The creation of organizational reality is not only limited by society and culture but also by the specifics of an individual's cognitive apparatus (perception via the senses and interpretation using the mind and language).

We can say that cognitive inspirations in management lead in different directions. In the interpretative trend, the cognitive process depends on the linguistic, cognitive, and cultural equipment of the individual and of social groups (the perspectives of the social sciences and the humanities). The reductionist trend attempts to derive categories of understanding reality, including the world of the organization, from neuronal dependencies.

Postmodernism is not a homogeneous trend; its concepts differ from one another, although they do of course have aspects in common. Undoubtedly, postmodernism has lost importance over the past decade, both in the social sciences and in management science. This argument can be illustrated by the number of publications on the topic of postmodernism in management (the phrase *postmodernism + management*) in the Google Scholar database. In the years 2000–2010, the database contained over 42,000 publications, while in the years 2011–2021, there were considerably fewer, with only 25,000 or so. In the last decade, there have also been considerably more texts critical of postmodernism in management and treating postmodernism as a stage preceding the emergence of the critical paradigm (*Critical Management Studies*).

Postmodernism reaches for the philosophy of scepticism and criticizes the possibility of achieving objective truth. Extreme cognitive relativism is also reflected in management (McKelvey 2003). A radical relativistic position is held by Bloor and Barnes, creators of the Edinburgh school of sociology of scientific knowledge, as we mentioned earlier. They do not treat science as a privileged cultural sphere. In their opinion, the way of perceiving reality and the criteria of rationality and truth depend on society and culture, and theories are the expression of social ideologies. The experiences hidden in culture are the basis for beliefs, new experiences, and the aims of interest groups, which make up the state of knowledge, the effect of cultural convention. We are condemned to moral and social relativism.

Similar views on the cultural entanglement of science are expressed by Feyerabend, who along with Foucault led to the rise of the sceptical trend with regard to science. Science and knowledge interpreted through the lens of control and symbolic violence. For representatives of the radical trend, scientific revolutions meant a complete departure from previous paradigms – there is no such thing as a 'core of knowledge' transferred through experience, the terms have new meanings, and there is also no cognitive principle, for example, rationality or any framework for creating knowledge. Since 'everything is allowed', there are no limitations on scientific theories and methodological anarchy rules. Feyerabend condemned scientific imperialism for colonizing religion and ethics. In acquiring an ethical aspect, science served to enslave both social groups and weaker cultures. The choice of scientific tradition is ideological in nature, as its products can have both good and bad applications. Science can therefore constitute one of many options, but it should not be considered as a criterion for assessing the value of cultural phenomena.

Foucault linked the issues of cognition and knowledge with power and drew attention to the circulation of power in the network. In his opinion, the link between power and knowledge is permanent, as in ruling over others we create truth. He is the author of the concept of the archaeology of knowledge, a method of historical analysis devoid of a subject, leading to the revealing of power mechanisms correlated with cognitive mechanisms. He looked into how, with the help of science (medicine), power influenced the concept of mental illness and shaped procedures for dominance over individuals not submitting to discipline. Such examples allow us to draw the conclusion that knowledge enables individuals to rule over others as well as the move from physical to symbolic violence. The truth no longer constitutes an overriding value and does not have to be linked to good; therefore, it is no longer above morality – ethics and science are equal to one another.

Postmodernists approach the achievements of European science sceptically. According to Polonai (1958), engaged post-critical philosophy is right, not trends whose ideal is the search for rational knowledge. The source of knowledge in the culturalist perspective embedded in postmodernism is passion, silent knowledge, and the community of language. Abandoning the desire for objectivism causes the individual to accept responsibility for their beliefs, while also enriching ethical knowledge. A criticism of science also appears in Lyotard's work, for whom the European tradition, along with epistemological, ethical, and cognitive universals, is merely a 'great illusion' and a 'metanarrative' – attempts to outdo universality and put cognitive discourse first seem unfounded. Reality is created by various, often conflicting discourses. Lyotard speaks straightforward about entering moral discourse into the cognitive act and emphasizes its role. According to postmodernism, the researcher of the organization uses the Wittgenstein concept of 'language game' but recognizes the untranslatability of games and the heterogeneity of discourses. Lyotard also notes the link between knowledge and power, the economization of science.

Knowledge is a resource and a tool of domination, dependent on the principles of economic efficiency. Modernism disregards sciences that do not gather knowledge or submit to technological transformation. The hope of unity in cognitive discourse vanished along with the metanarratives of the hermeneutics of meaning (historicism), the teleology of the spirit (idealism), and also the emancipation of humankind (enlightenment). Science has its own rules that gave the impression of empirical verification. Procedures were created, but discourse found itself above the rules and adopted efficiency as a criterion of the success of science. The efficiency of language games is revealed when its rules lead to economic efficiency in practice. The discourses find themselves in a conflict situation, and consensus is achieved in only one discourse, which is therefore of a local nature. According to Lyotard, the diversity and incommensurability of discourses have social and ethical consequences, lead to a rejection of fundamentalism, do not allow for discourses to be subject to uniform economic reasoning, indicate a high degree of tolerance, and at the same time adopt a critical stance. Of course, justice still exists, and all discourse participants should have the possibility to express views. Lyotardian postmodernist thinking assumes the co-existence of various cultural discourses in conditions of relativism. Science does not have a dominating role; it is divided into language games and can be criticized within another discourse.

What postmodernist concepts can be adapted for management? Certainly neopragmatism, which assumes cognition oriented towards action. Rorty (2010) considers philosophy based on the search for the truth to be worn out and limiting. From the Platonic concept of ideas arose the concept of the mind, described by Rorty (2007) using the metaphor of a mirror, as the mind reflects reality in a similar fashion. What Rorty finds infertile in epistemology is the assumption that in cognition it is about the accuracy of presentation, sanctioning the cognitive aspirations of science. Fundamentalism, which reduces philosophy to epistemology, is mistaken in the researcher's opinion, as the mind is not a mirror reflecting reality. In the neopragmatist approach, concepts are tools of effective action, consisting of all available knowledge used by humankind to make life better.

There are no systemic ambitions here; knowledge, as a social and cultural creation, is at the service of action, not universal cognition. The truth is created, not discovered and is the effect of social mediation. Rorty (2007) criticizes the concept of the main trend as epistemological fundamentalism and prefers radical non-fundamentalist philosophies, in which cognition is no longer the most important, nor even an autonomous human activity. Radical anti-fundamentalism is also characterized by anti-essentialism, that is the elimination of metaphysical elements from science, contained in the concepts of 'truth' and 'cognition'. They are replaced by an assumption about relationality, knowledge existing in context. Concepts are created by relating them to human needs, consciousness, or language, and the inner nature of things cannot be known.

In Rorty's (2007) pragmatic-hermeutic theses, concepts are cognitively and culturally relative. Persistent relativism leads to rejecting epistemology and basing science only on practice. The philosopher is no longer a 'supervisor of culture', proficient in cognitive criteria, but a 'Socratic mediator', an interpreter, trying to find their place in the translatability of discourses and in creating effective tools, that is concepts. The scientific community is not united around one 'universitas' aim, but 'societas', that is a group of people connected by sociability and the intersection of life's paths. The consequence of understanding culture as a conversation is holism, according to which everyone has the right to create their own paradigm (i.e. language game).

Rorty (2007), on the basis of analogy to Kuhn's normal and revolutionary science, divides discourses into:

- Normal – a set of conventions naming the features of valuable knowledge and the appropriate type of argumentation (e.g. the rationality type). Participants develop common theorems;

- Non-normal – occurring in new situations, devoid of conventions, with incommensurable concepts. The effect can equally be a meaningful sentence as well as a paradox.

The acceptance of neopragmatic rules in management would involve recognition that the aim of management is to create reality, not its reproduction and that its methods are constructivist in nature, contributing to changes in reality – not always in accordance with the intention of the researcher, as change can be spontaneous and uncontrolled. Organization and management can therefore be interpreted in many different ways, including contradictory ones. This thinking is evident in management in metaphors, paradoxes, organization archetypes, and the trend of organizational spirituality. Another manifestation of neopragmatism in management is the abandonment of holistic and systemic thinking. The adoption in management of extreme cultural and epistemological relativism (*de facto* the most important feature of postmodernism) has serious consequences:

1 Management becomes a local science; therefore, investigations are conducted in the cultural context and are subjective, and generalizations and transfers cannot be extended to other cases. The variability of cultural conditions translates into conflicting cultural discourses within management itself, which is why its principles cannot be applied to various cultures. The locality of management is linked to its social context and the untranslatability of concepts. However, in criticizing postmodernism, it is worth noting that the untranslatability of discourses from various cultural contexts is not entirely confirmed by reality. Some management problems are cross-cultural and could be called universal, for example, exercising power, building teams, and organizing work efficiently. The ways for solving these problems differ and depend on political, social, and economic factors. In my opinion, they can also be transferred to other cultures, although this is not easy and is not devoid of limitations. Examples include scientific management techniques, total quality management (TQM), and shaping leadership and organizational culture.
2 Postmodernist management would have to reject cognitive universalism and scientific ambitions, adopt the theses of neopragmatism, and focus on individual cultural studies. Drucker compared management to medicine, which is a science but makes use of the achievements of other sciences – management would appear to do the same. Cognitive relativism and the abandonment of theoretical ambitions would entail the liquidation of the cognitive foundations of management, which would mean the abandonment of scientific ambitions, although it would still exist as a practice.
3 Postmodernists consider that the desire to improve the organization at the cost of society contains remnants of imperialism. The belief in scientific principles of ideal management is naturally an illusion. The creators of concepts or methods in management seem to sometimes forget that social and

economic practice is based not only on theoretical knowledge but also on intuition and experience and is therefore a science, a craft, and an art. For this reason, postmodernist management can be a neopragmatistic reflection on the organization but without imposing solutions on its members. Theorists and practitioners are equally important and can communicate with one another.

4 Management science has at its disposal a huge number of social institutions (academic centres, research groups) as well as graduates of many different varieties of management. However, social institutions are often merely bureaucratic structures stimulating demand for their own intellectual products. Postmodernist authors proclaim the dependency of the content of management on the social context. Empirical verification methods, scientific facts, and theories are created in academic or consulting centres and are therefore closed in discourses that, along with the growth of the scientific community, divide into specific branches. Many subdisciplines are incommensurable, with one language being used by company financial managers and a different one used by those responsible for marketing. This is not indicative of the existence of various paradigms and groups of theories but points to the development of the management environment, which has led to variations in language and the issues at stake. The sociological approach to the creation of knowledge in management should explain how the scientific community creates a demand for its knowledge as well as for social significance and power. It would be interesting to analyse how management discourses absorb various issues, underlining their own importance. Such professional centrism builds an ideology of management as an effective science and practice. Management, like many social sciences, is entangled in language, and discourses have linguistic foundations. The criterion for accepting or rejecting a given concept is often a matter of belief, not scientific argumentation. The task of management is to deconstruct its own basic concepts and cognitive methods, while at the same time granting consent for the ambiguity of concepts, the definitions of the organization or its elements, which become 'language games'. Attempts to create universal dictionaries in management are simply examples of local discursive consensuses.

5 Power constitutes a significant problem in management and is addressed by both the critical trend and postmodernism. Power is a component of organizational relationships; however, exercising power can become ethically controversial and may mean the use of violence, not usually physical of course but symbolic. Postmodernist management features ethical and social sensitivity.

6 A radical postmodernist orientation that rejects universal values makes it impossible to practice management as a science. This can be seen in the consequences of the theses of Rorty, the Edinburgh school and Lyotard. For these reasons, the radical anti-epistemology of postmodernism cannot constitute the basis for organization and management science. However, a moderate

postmodernist approach is characterized by a scientific scepticism that can be used in multi-paradigm sciences such as management.

The postmodernist trend plays a creative, critical, and aesthetic role; however, it has not become an epistemological alternative. The critical function allows us to bring to light the apparent cognitive foundations of management, raise doubts as to the realistic vision of the organization in the systemic interpretation, emphasize the entanglement of management in the ideology of power, and question the objectivism of reflecting reality in the process of its cognition. The relativistic approach has replaced cognitive absolutism. The researcher is someone who makes a significant intervention in the object being studied, and this perspective can therefore be inspiring for many management researchers.

Postmodernism underlines the necessity for multiple understandings of organizational reality in management. This is expressed in the departure from 'epistemological fundamentalism' to the benefit of 'pluralism' or 'epistemological anarchy'. Thanks to moderate postmodernism, the methodological sphere often makes use of metaphors, paradoxes, and images of the organization from other disciplines, which can only enrich the view of the organization and management. Postmodernism is marginalized in contemporary management science discourse. However, it will only be possible to assess the value of inspiration from postmodernist thinking in the long term.

The social sciences feature self-reflection in terms of their own theories, methods, and basic cognitive assumptions. Management science sporadically conducts a critical examination of even their epistemological foundations. The sources of the critical trend are:

- The Frankfurt school;
- Neo-Marxism;
- Postmodernism;
- Concepts of performativity;
- Textualism;
- A strong programme of the sociology of knowledge;
- Feminism.

The critical trend in management science assumes a radical vision of the development of the organization, which constitutes a tool of domination and oppression. Its background includes neo-Marxism, beginning with Karl Marx's class struggle, to the criticism of the consumer society and the mass media postulated in the Frankfurt school, in particular by Habermas (Scherer 2009). Further significant sources are poststructuralism and postmodernism, with Foucault discussing the issue of power and domination. Other supporters of cognitive and cultural relativism who had an influence on the development of the critical trend are Jameson, Rorty, Derrida, Baudrillard, and Bauman. Another source of a social movement nature with a cognitive perspective is radical feminism, whose aim is the struggle against the existing order based on patriarchal power relationships. In the last decade, following on from neopragmatistic postulates of the inseparable connection between the process of cognition and action, CMS also assimilates the concept of performativity. We can therefore say that the CMS trend has a very rich and heterogeneous intellectual background, although it constitutes a new perspective as its beginnings reach back to the 1990s, with the publication of the work *Critical Management Studies* by Alvesson and Willmott. The first works, related to ideological demystification and based on the structures of the dominance of management functions, were published in the 1970s, while the institutionalized trend has existed for the past 30 years, with the appearance of publications, conferences, research, journals, and associations (such as the CMS Academy of Management).

This perspective belongs to the group of alternative paradigms (such as interpretivism and postmodernism), whose identity is shaped in opposition to the dominating NFS paradigm. Their common assumptions are, for example:

- The key role in management of the distribution of power and communication;
- An interpretative and processual vision of organizing;
- Cultural relativism;
- The dominance of qualitative methods.

What distinguishes between these paradigms? The differences can be seen in Burrell and Morgan's (1979) interpretation of the paradigm matrix. The IS paradigm features subjectivism and focuses on a descriptive and local way of conducting cognitive discourse, while CMS is about a quasi-objective description of unfair practices in organizations and how to change them. The similarities between CMS and postmodernism are even greater, as they are linked by the issue of power, the oppressiveness of social structures, and the use of textualism and criticism of modernity. However, postmodernism is subjectivist, while CMS wants to reveal and change real, objectively or quasi-objectively existing relationships of domination. Postmodernism has become anti-methodological and uses only individual studies, while CMS has adopted and shapes qualitative and engaged methodology.

Management science constitutes here a persuasive discourse, drawing on capitalism and striving to maintain the current status with the mechanisms of domination and exploitation. The critical trend aims to question the only apparently 'objective' and 'natural' organizational order, management power, institutions, practices, and managerial identities (Alvesson, Willmott 2003). Under the guise of the rationality of management science hide actions that are oppressive and damaging to society; the critical trend strives to describe them and to 'denaturalize' managerialism.

Apart from criticism of the existing order, the revealing of the interests of groups in power, also through control of the scientific discourse, leads to a change in this order. The development of the critical trend aims to allow disadvantaged groups (women, ethnic, and social minorities) to express and achieve their interests. In addition to their emancipation, the mechanisms of symbolic violence would be discovered, and instrumental managerial practices would be abandoned (Verduijn et al. 2014, p. 98). Tools of the critical trend include:

- Deconstruction and denaturalization of managerial discourse;
- Methods for strengthening autonomy and self-control among disadvantaged groups (e.g. *empowerment*);
- Methods for increasing participation in decision-making bodies (e.g. parity);
- Analysis of the language of exercising power.

Management cannot exist without certain institutional frameworks. In recent years, academic institutions have striven to break with hierarchy and to be flexible and open to change; however, they often feature centralized, fossilized structures. In such institutions, symbolic power consists of creating scientific norms. According to the critical trend, this power should be verified so that science is valuable and not monopolized.

Currently, knowledge is not so much a 'selfless pursuit of truth' but a tool in the hands of the people in power; theories depend on political and economic power. We can also see this in management science, whose aim was to create conditions for the efficient operation of organizations, which most often included companies and also non-commercial institutions, including oppressive ones (the police, the army).

In the critical trend, management sanctions the manipulation of organization members and the consideration of theories as objective truths. The theory of scientific management rationalized organizations' instrumental treatment of employees (e.g. their dismissal using methods such as *job sharing* or *reengineering*). *TQM* can contribute to the rationalization of power in the organization and the managerial discourse thanks to the reproduction of ideology and perpetuating false consciousness among employees. In management, there is a belief in the necessity and salvation of globalization, without answering the question who will really benefit from it.

Management, as a normative science, is supposed to develop principles of organization and support business practice, which of course is the case, but it does not constitute a standard. A businessperson or manager does not need management training, but applying the principles developed by the discipline in practice is of great importance. For this reason, the academic community strives to prove the value of applying their proposed theories; however, these do not always work in practice.

Consulting activities have emerged between the business and academic sectors that are intended to serve managers and are maintained thanks to the application of management theories, which is why they also strive to sustain the influence of management science (which does not always preserve its cognitive authority). In spite of this, it must be admitted that consulting does to a large extent carry out the transfer of research results into management practice, creating a feedback loop between theory and practice. Theoretical postulates, which are supposed to have an impact on practice, may be ideologically motivated or serve the aims of interested groups.

The more important interest groups include entrepreneurs, owners, consultants, and scientists – specialists in management, while the 'prizes' in the ongoing social game are prestige, power, financial resources, and the possibility to achieve strategic missions and aims. Here, we can of course make social divisions (private-public sector) or national divisions as well as indicate other motivators (such as the feeling of security). The interests of the above groups overlap in a complex configuration of more or less conscious and permanent coalitions. These may hide behind the veil of a claim to objectivity. This social game also functions in management. Managers are one of the most important groups as it is they who control financial resources and services as well as have power in the majority of social structures, often greater than that of political decision-makers. Managerialism has even entered the public sector, as claimed by representatives of CMS (Hudon, Rouillard 2015, pp. 527–548). Managers create their own ideology so as to reinforce and rationalize their position. This ideology creates group identity and solidarity and is also visible in the subject concepts and in management methods developed in the dominating trend.

Management science draws on instrumental rationalism. Management processes are about efficient organization of work based on scientific, objective principles. The cognitive aims of management science translate into the pragmatics of managers' actions. The roles of executive and manager are the basic subject of interest of our discourse. Management according to the main trend leads to the creation of an idealized picture of their actions. The description of decision-making processes in the firm has its roots in the assumptions of *homo oeconomicus* and would appear to disregard the influence of the social group.

The perception of management as an ideology rationalizing power is present in all threads of the critical trend. From this emerges the social self of the manager, emphasizing the pursuit of success, the rationality of action, utilitarianism, pragmatism, loyalty to the institution, and belief in the managerial ethos. The critical trend considers that these components of the manager's identity merely justify their efforts to dominate others.

Maintaining a self-reproducing social order, created thanks to managerial power, is not possible without symbolic violence. Those who submit to such violence must first agree with the institutions of ownership and the market. This is the aim that management serves, in other words a system for the rationalization of social domination, operating under the cover of science and social practice. Harding claims that a system for the social legitimization of power has developed in management, comprising the academic community, business schools, and business publishers. Thanks to symbolic violence, the following assumptions are present in social discourse:

- Management uncovers the truth about reality.
- Management is an art that enables power to be exercised over others.
- Without management, the world would be in chaos (Harding 2003, p. 14).

Continuing the topic of the ideological nature of management, it is worth reaching for the Marxist thread of false consciousness, constructed by the education system, which replicates the ideological knowledge of management. Supporters of *Critical Management Education* consider that business schools 'enslave the minds' of owners and employees by suggesting sources of identity to them. We achieve false consciousness when we identify with an apparently objective, scientific, and just system for exercising power. This system is created for the benefit of the dominant social group and becomes a tool of control. In soliciting services and things, people contribute to the development of transnational corporations and the success of managers at the highest level. False consciousness is not only a feature of managers, ensuring them a feeling of mission and justice, but also of employees and consumers. Managerial education of an indoctrinatory nature has an influence on the reproduction of power.

We know that management does not create a single paradigm, set of theories and methodologies, but a mixture of various concepts of ever shorter duration. Most often, they are not based on research but on an idea that simplifies organizational reality. The rapid spread of a concept is talked about and also its abandonment by organizations and management theorists. Fashionable theories increase the popularity of management science at the cost of its credibility. These are an example of social constructivism, in which a concept has a return effect on organizational reality.

Management critics do a great deal to bring into question its 'scientificity', pointing to its ideological nature and the limited scope of theories and methods. However, many theses of the critical trend (e.g. management as a pseudoscience and as an ideology of domination) seem to be exaggerated and arbitrarily accepted. Acknowledging this criticism, it should be noted that everything depends on the criteria of 'scientificity'. If we compare management to the natural sciences by reaching for neopositivist ideals, we have to give a poor assessment of its cognitive effectiveness. However, if we compare it to the social sciences and the humanities, the discourse fulfils scientific criteria, as management is considered to be a science, functions in the scientific community and institutions, has a specific (although obviously ambiguous) subject of interest, its own research perspective, and also makes use of various cognitive perspectives and research methods. Accepting the conventional nature of the division between scientific disciplines and the commonality of the research problem in many sciences, we do not negate the status of 'scientificity' of management. This scientific credibility is not however devoid of value judgements and ideology. It is impossible not to notice the problems of a lack of ethics and domination raised by the critical trend, nor to explain them via universalism and scientific objectivism. Departing from the ideals of neopositivism means placing elements of ethics and cultural relativism in science. However, these should enrich the discourse, not deny its sense. The critical trend does not have to be associated with the destruction of management science but with its reconstruction. Instrumental rationalism, which constitutes its basis from the epistemological perspective, is uncompromising only in appearance. Taking into account the aspect of its humanization, management science concepts include the social responsibility of business, the sustainable development of enterprises, human capital, employee self-realization, and individuality as well as ideas that make use of alternative paradigms, such as diversity and *empowerment*. The problems concerning communicating in a group or exercising power are within the field of interest of various social sciences and also the humanities and the natural sciences, which means a multitude of points of view and the lack of a strict demarcation between the research issues addressed by the sciences as well as interdisciplinarity.

The above considerations do not undermine the cognitive value of management science, nor do they lead to the assertion that theories are only constructed in order to achieve the interests of influential groups and that all management content is socially conditioned. However, they constitute an attempt to analyse the effects of ideology on management and are an important source of reflection on the influence of interest groups on the processes of creating knowledge. Research on discriminated groups in particular areas of management may help in revealing the mechanisms of legitimizing social power using the appearance of rationality. Naturally, the cultural and social context are not the only source of knowledge. However, when there is a lack of direct access to the studied reality, interpretations are related to the social context (interests, culture) (Sage, Dainty, Brookes 2014, pp. 544–555).

The lack of universality of knowledge in management discourse or the social stimulation of its development (through the influence of power, conflicts of interest, the scientific community) sensitize us to the problem of the conditions for content and the means of achieving knowledge in our science, which is very important in the context of the credibility of creating social sciences. Criticism of CMS is characterized by radicalism, and its provocative approach to basic management problems encourages polemics. Of course, the concepts of this trend differ from one another but they are connected by cognitive criticism and the ethical side of management, which may lead to radical changes in our discourse. Following a general analysis of the CMS paradigm, it would be good to relate its theses to various subdisciplines of management science.

Part II

Reevaluation of Current Paradigms in Management Science

5 What Is a Paradigm Shifts in Management Science?

It is difficult to clearly define the subject of management science. The areas of interest in the discipline focus not only on understanding and improving the organization but also on the actions of people within the organization and outside it. The history of the discipline shows that it is usually connected to Western civilizations, which in recent centuries have held control over the dominant world organizations (Frenkel, Shenhav 2006, pp. 855–876). The blurring of the subject of management science and the crossover with research fields in various disciplines are testimony to the dynamic development of our discourse. Paradigm shifts in management science can lead to the emergence of new theories, frameworks, and practices that better align with the current realities of the business environment.

Embracing paradigm shifts in management science is essential for organizations to remain agile, innovative, and competitive in an ever-changing global landscape. At various stages of its development, management science has made use of concepts and methods from the technical sciences, the humanities, the economics, and the natural sciences. This has had positive effects in the form of the openness and even inclusivity of the discipline and also negative effects due to the weak demarcation from related sciences (Badea 2013, pp. 179–187). Paradigm shifts represent transformative changes in fundamental beliefs, assumptions, and approaches within a particular field of study or practice. These shifts often occur when existing paradigms fail to adequately explain or address new discoveries, challenges, or societal changes. Paradigm shifts can originate from scientific breakthroughs, technological advancements, cultural shifts, or philosophical reconsiderations.

Let us begin chronologically – the first source, still currently in use in the scientific trend of management, is the technical sciences (Andres, Dobrovská 2015, pp. 99–101). Here, the organization is understood in a material sense; it is subject to processes of optimalisation in the management system. The research approach is objectivist and pragmatic; the methodology is based on processes: designing, monitoring, and supervision. Historically, the second inspirational trend is economics. In this approach, it is recommended to combine limited rationalism

DOI: 10.4324/9781003530947-8

with market orientation in striving to achieve profits thanks to implemented economic undertakings. The deductive view is linked to a preference for statistical methods.

Inspiration from the natural sciences is also visible in management, in particular neopositivist and systems concepts, the striving for monism in science, and objective, verifiable knowledge acquired thanks to the scientific method. Neopositivism did not create its own school in management but influenced the sociological, engineering, and economic trends. Its assumptions were continued by the systems school. From the natural sciences (from Darwinism to be precise) emerged behavioural economics and neo-evolutionism, which contains elements of evolutionary psychology (Leydesdorff 2021, pp. 89–113). The humanities were also a source of inspiration (especially psychological and sociological thinking). Organization and management were seen here as intersubjective psychosocial processes, classified using various methods and cognitive perspectives.

Striving to integrate scientific problems and methods around research fields and problems is an argument for using the positions of various sciences. A hierarchy of fields and areas was created on the basis of convention, largely academic or social, and research problems are often independent of discipline boundaries.

Epistemological and methodological inspirations may help in developing new scientific solutions which could not be attempted within a single discipline. Using the potential of other disciplines is an example of the creative approach, which merely requires a certain distance and reflection. Here, I understand reflectiveness as the adapting of concepts to the specifics of our discourse (Cassell, Radcliffe, Malik 2020, pp. 750–773) – nothing can be transferred mechanically or overly simplified. It becomes necessary to understand the source methodology, which after all has its own specifics. Researchers must be aware of both the limitations of ways of cognition and the metaphorical process of transposing concepts and theories from other disciplines. The belief that methods can be transferred literally results in exhausting the possibilities of a given perspective or metaphor. The hypostasis error has already occurred in management, in the engineering approach, and in cultural functionalism. Literal adoption of concepts from other disciplines left them empty or reduced them to the role of a metaphor in management. Some concepts and methods were treated literally and became sterile, while they could have been cognitively useful if only they had been treated critically and reflexively.

Examples of inspiration from other sciences include the concept of organizational learning, establishing organizational reality, organizational culture, identity and personality, emergent strategies, and postmodernism in management.

The examples presented above of the influence of various scientific fields on management provide us with a picture of an interdisciplinary science that must have its own cognitive autonomy in order to shape its own identity. The problem of demarcation is no stranger to any science, in particular the social sciences. This is often understood as indicating clear and permanent boundaries between the sciences. Defining the boundaries that separate management science from other fields of science (in particular sociology, social psychology and economics) is exceptionally problematic, resulting in endless discussions in the field.

To take a position in this regard, it is necessary to reach for ontological, epistemological, methodological, and institutional arguments. At the ontological level, the argument will be the assumption that the level of organizing and managing processes differs from other spheres of reality. This is correct in the case of differences between the social world and the natural world but not necessarily in the case of the field of the social sciences itself. In the latter field, the reflective subject comes to the fore, shaping the reality being described. Interpersonal cooperation, the exercising of power, communication, and decision-making do not belong exclusively to one science – they remain universal in nature and occur not only in all management sciences but also in sociology, economics, and anthropology. It is therefore difficult to accept the ontological foundations for the emergence of management science on the basis of the nature of reality.

The epistemological argument talks of indicating the distinctiveness of management science by means of the subject of research. Similarly to the previous case, it is easy to notice the differences between the social and the natural sciences – they differ in terms of the subject of research, the approach, the researcher's orientation, and heuristics. These differences are clearly visible; nevertheless, some researchers accept without reserve the cognitive ideals of the natural sciences. This leads to a questionable scientistic attitude. Therefore, the differentiation of epistemological criteria in the social sciences also turns out to be problematic – differences can of course be found, but many of these sciences have common research fields.

It is hard to identify a clear and specific subject of research in management science. The simplest approach – as a study of management processes – does not mean a complete separation of our discourse from other social sciences. Management encompasses not only people but also organizations and social groups (thus also political parties and the state). The methodological argument would be to find a method developed in a given discipline as well as a research subject and research approach. However, management science adapts methods and techniques from other sciences and is thus polymethodical, which is the next argument why it is not possible to make a clear demarcation between it and the other social sciences.

The institutional argument is about finding distinctiveness in one's own academic institutions that reflects the development of the scientific discipline. There has certainly been a proliferation of business schools that have produced a huge number of management graduates. Academic staff have also received new development opportunities, with numerous publications bearing testament to their scientific achievements. However, the distinction between the identity of a management theorist and practitioner is still blurred. Of course, there is no lack of specialists dealing with management issues (mostly on the boundaries of disciplines). However, in the management science community there is a lack of social reproduction, in particular in Poland, although not only. Specialists are more likely to laud their education in psychology, sociology, economics, mathematics, anthropology, and even philosophy. Interestingly, the profession of management science specialist does not even have a name. After all, a scientist or researcher is not the same as an entrepreneur or businessperson. Professional identity is transferred to the fulfilling of various functions in organizations. Professional groups from management science include marketing and logistics specialists, accountants, and HR specialists, but all these groups are characterized by high distinctiveness and homogeneity of identity.

The institutional difficulty in defining the boundaries of management science is also visible in scientific policy, for example, in disputes related to confirming the title of habilitated doctor in cases where the committee members consider the affiliation to the discipline to be questionable.

These institutional problems also appear to be a consequence of the epistemological features of management science, that is the overlap of methods, research approaches, and research subject in various sciences. It is not possible to precisely determine the subject and place of management science in the institutional sense while maintaining blurred epistemological categories. This would result in impoverishing management science. In such an approach, only specific management issues would belong to the science, such as those related to decision-making by managers in organizations, while 'peripheral' issues, of which there are considerably more than those we can consider to be core, would be rejected. And it is here that we often find to most creative solutions. How can we then solve problems related to the institutional assessment of scientific achievements? The most important criterion should certainly be that of quality, not discipline purity. Disciplinary 'purism' and attempts at artificial demarcation lead to key interdisciplinary issues being omitted in research. An effective unit parametrization system, as well as interdisciplinary assessment of scientific achievements, should provide the answer to dilemmas related to conducting scientific evaluation.

If we take into consideration arguments of an institutional and cognitive nature (epistemological and methodological), it would appear that a position of weak distinction of management science is more justified. This involves the interdisciplinarity of methods and research approaches and the encroaching of management issues into the domain of other sciences. Management is still a separate scientific discipline with a specific institutional form, and whose theories are constantly developing. This is related to the tension between management practice and normative definitions.

Some areas of management may be characterized by greater demarcation from other sciences than others; however, problems that are shared with other social sciences will certainly emerge during the research process. For this reason, I opt for a liberal understanding of management science, which constitutes the field of economic, social, and scientific practices dealt with by management theorists and practitioners. Critical assessment of its achievements using various cognitive perspectives would seem to be more important than searching for the boundaries of the science.

To sum up, the issue of demarcation can be solved by indicating the particular features of the research subject and its partial separation in comparison to other disciplines. Management science deals with the organized activity of people, taking into account socio-economic aspects. The core of the science related to the world of management is defined, while peripheral issues are debatable, although they do constitute an inseparable part of management. The strength of the theory of organization and management lies in its diversity. The inspiration for its subdisciplines may be economic (operational studies, management accounting), humanistic (organizational culture, HRM), or engineering (quality management, production, logistics). Therefore, two principal areas concentrating the issues can be indicated: humanistic and technical-economic. Let us consider this to be a permanent feature of the discipline, which constitutes 'boundary research fields'. Although the use of various perspectives does not provide a consistent picture of the organization, thanks to such an approach the importance of the problems addressed by the science can be identified. Let the core of management science be a signpost guiding researchers who reach the peripheries. The applied concepts will enrich our knowledge of the world of the organization. One specific problem may not belong to one specific discipline. The fogginess of the boundaries of management science is a source of not only institutional problems but also creative solutions – which is why I choose the position of weak distinction. What solutions do I find in the face of the need for the demarcation of disciplines and the interdisciplinary problems of the life of the organization? I certainly consider it important that a broad discussion be conducted in the scientific community on the identity of management science, while at the same time accepting the fact that its boundaries are not clear and that research fields overlap. I also propose the selection of criteria for assessment of the quality of scientific research depending on research problems, not disciplines. In assessing concepts, let us assess their value, not whether they belong to the discourse. It is also necessary to identify criteria for the quality of interdisciplinary scientific achievements. It would be good to strengthen the identity of management science researchers and support scientists working on the value added of the discipline.

6 Understanding Paradigm Shifts

The development of every science is accompanied by cognitive crises, which contribute to increasing epistemological awareness and at the same time greater cognitive effectiveness. A crisis manifests itself in a move away from existing ways of conducting science as well as criticism towards the methods used and the results of research. Neither the natural sciences nor the social sciences and humanities have avoided a cognitive crisis (Gouldner 1970; Fleck 1986, pp. 153–158). There are many symptoms and causes of crises in science. These can relate to a general fall in the level of trust in science, research, and experts, combined with an increase in the belief in unverified information disseminated by unreliable sources (Saltelli, Ravetz, Funtowicz 2016, pp. 1–30). In the social sciences, the latest serious crisis is connected to a rejection of many concepts, especially in psychology, due to the lack of repeatability of research results that allowed the phenomenon to be described.

Due to the rapid institutional and social development in management science, a crisis was unavoidable. Researchers involved in conducting their own analyses sometimes fail to see the seriousness of questioning the cognitive foundations of a scientific discipline. Many aspects of the crisis have already appeared in our considerations. We know that researchers do not agree on the fundamental concepts of management science. We are still unsure whether to understand the organization attributively, factually, or functionally. There is a growing number of approaches, models, and organizational metaphors that are not subject to empirical verification. Can we in any way speak of 'organizing'? The subject of cognition may not exist, it may also be more complex than in other discourses, or maybe the cognitive question has been posed incorrectly. Management does not make use of a single universal scientific theory, which does not mean that it does not have data from cognitively valuable research. Quite the opposite – there is a large amount of data, but the difficulty is in comparing and assessing its cognitive value. In management, the relations between theory and practice as well as between its descriptive and normative status have not been resolved. The latter strives to indicate rules for an entity's effective action in a given situation. Identifying all situational conditions is no longer that important. This differs from

DOI: 10.4324/9781003530947-9

the descriptive approach, in which the researcher wants to describe reality and explain all the variables but does not interfere in them nor become an organizer.

Management is also accompanied by a permanent crisis of the repeatability of research results, the majority of which are situational and difficult to re-verify. As I mentioned earlier, this is not exclusively a problem of management but is a relatively common phenomenon in the social sciences and the humanities. Management also does not possess its own methods but develops thanks to the adaptation of methods and techniques from other sciences, which is why the discipline is sometimes accused of being immature. As has been proven, it is not possible to completely distinguish management from other scientific disciplines due to the common fields of research. Interdisciplinarity is also expressed in institutional changes in the academic structure as well as in the division of scientific fields and disciplines, which brings the threat of its disintegration. An example of the weak demarcation of management from other disciplines can be seen in the latest move in the ephemeral direction of 'management and quality science'. We are already aware of all this – but what is the effect of this self-critical cognitive reflection?

Comparing the traditions of philosophy and the social sciences may lead to the conclusion that such a cognitive shockwave may be stimulating and facilitating the differentiation of valuable knowledge from symptoms of cognitive pathology and pseudo-theory. The 'universal truths' that appear in increasingly popular management handbooks contribute to building its image as a merely apparent science, in which the commercial sphere rather than cognitive aspects play the principal role. Of course, it is important not to negate the value of very many new research projects, but management would appear to be in great need of reliable and critical reflection.

How can the crisis in management science be overcome? Undoubtedly, this may be helped by acceptance of the assumptions of epistemological pluralism, with its clear criteria for cognitive value. Below, we present postulates that may constitute a way in which to overcome the crisis.

1 Management science should not be driven by universalist ambitions; it is worth focusing on local discourse and its creative aspects. Our discipline, grounded historically, socially, and culturally, has not, like many other social sciences and humanities, generated universal, synthetic theories. It is likely that the concentration on medium- and short-term theories, local discourses, and situational results will turn out to be long-lasting. Knowledge in management science is only approximate and uncertain and is subject to influences from the cultural, social, and historical context, which manifests itself in the effect of value on cognition, the cognitive role of language, and the adoption of historical criteria of rationality (that is cultural relativism). Management is placed in a hermeneutic circle, that is the cognitive and linguistic apparatus can also change depending on the ways reality is interpreted (Sułkowski

2015, 2016). Of course, we cannot completely ignore non-cultural sources of knowledge, and while intercultural knowledge should also be made use of, it cannot be considered to be universal, although it does constitute a certain compromise solution.

2 Management should draw on other scientific disciplines. In the natural sciences and the humanities, there is no lack of concepts that can become the source of fundamental theories or medium-term theories used to interpret the processes of organizing and management. For example, the neo-evolutionary paradigm can be helpful in analysing the behaviour of people in the organization. The transfer between discourses should be subject to epistemological analysis; concepts can be used literally or metaphorically. Care should be taken in using analogies with the natural world, as the world of humans and the organization is intersubjective, not objective.

   The concepts and paradigms do not meet – cannot meet – the assumptions of universalism. In management science we have diverse research problems, some of which were formed on the boundary between management and other disciplines, which is why openness to cognitive inspirations from other sciences would appear to be creative. It is similar with research approaches – various epistemological perspectives merely enrich the social sciences. Technical approaches allow for the manipulation of technologies, which increases individuals' effectiveness. The pragmatic approach focuses on communication and creating the culture and structure of power, which aim to facilitate cooperation between people. The reflexive approach enables critical analysis of the effects of implementing both approaches – technical and pragmatic. For this reason, eclecticism seems to be appropriate, combining various approaches, both cognitive and epistemological.

3 The scientistic orientation originating in neopositivism should not be promoted on the basis of management science, as it attempts to impose one 'scientific method' on social disciplines. The cognitive process in management is co-created in subjective processes of interpretation; it is not merely a reflection of reality but becomes reflexive, close to dialogue and hermeneutic. The people creating it are characterized by self-awareness and are able to change under the influence of the interpretations made. Management science is also a reflexive cognitive and practical activity. Scientific rationality can be used in its analysis, but not in an orthodox way as in neopositivism, but moderately, reaching for epistemological critique of the philosophy of science. It is worth searching for temporary cognitive and practical problems, without defining them as certain or universal. The search for a cognitive compromise that agrees on a pragmatic plane of joint actions leads to 'dialogical' science, in which one can communicate and interpret meanings in different ways. Cognition consists of creating the social world thanks to social and cognitive aspects, not merely reflecting it. The entity participates in this creation in its every action, entering into relations with other entities and forming a

reflexive and intersubjective perspective for understanding and building the world of the organization and management. Of course, this is not extreme constructivism, reality has its own specific features (Norris, Sawyer 2012).

4 The intertwining of management with practice also means co-creation of the studied reality. In practical activity, only intuitive and everyday categories are primary, language is already their interpretation. The management researcher intervenes in the research material, making planned and spontaneous changes, while the practitioner also cognizes organizational reality. The roles of the management researcher and practitioner are therefore interdependent.

5 In management science, rationalization and the pursuit of efficiency are connected with reinforcing the power of experts and technocrats. It is not without reason that managerialism is called the ideology of control (Deetz 1995, p. 4). Therefore, a critical analysis of the context of cognition is necessary.

7 Radical Paradigm Shifts

Criticism of traditional cultures, considered to be patriarchal, led to the emergence of feminism, which postulated the need to transform social structures in order to achieve equality for women, preceded by an unmasking of the masculinist mechanisms of power (socialization, language and discourse, and physical as well as symbolic violence) and epistemology (Oakley 2000; Hines 2019, pp. 145–157). According to Keller, the currently dominating epistemology is driven by the masculinist obsession with control over the life of the individual. Science as a tool of exercising power over life leads, for example, to the development of genetics or military science (Keller 1993). Radical feminism encourages the building of a new feminist epistemology that can change the cognitive perspective (Longino 2017, pp. 325–353). The revolution would take place not only in science but also in culture and the social structure. Harding gives three different 'feminist epistemologies' depending on their understanding of the nature of knowledge and its relations with issues of gender (Harding 1986).

1 Feminist empiricism – the least radical, as it does not negate the model of scientific cognition as such (with the use of the correspondence theory of truth, the scientific method, and the cumulation of achievements) but perceives its entanglement in sexism and patriarchy. In scientific practice we are faced with a lower participation of women (not only in science but also in other power structures), the adoption of masculinist arguments and a disregard for discrimination against women. Feminist empiricism assumes an increase in the participation of women in influence groups and science, the conducting of research on feminist issues, and the abandonment of masculinist theories (Kantola, Squires 2012, pp. 382–400). It deviates from the stereotype of an objective researcher, especially in the social sciences. It recognizes the cumulation of scientific achievements, but the criteria for their creation are community-based and social. To date, the consequence of the domination of science and power structures has been the masculinist accumulation of the achievements of the social sciences.

DOI: 10.4324/9781003530947-10

2 The feminist position – criticism of scientific achievements, the order maintained by the dominating social class, and the description of rational and just reality from the neo-Marxist perspective. To retain power, the dominating social class maintains the existing order and perceives and describes reality as rational, just and natural. In representatives of the discriminated group (here: women), false consciousness is created. The feminist avantgarde can awaken the consciousness of this group. The task of the researcher is to understand and criticize social mechanisms and then to change social reality thanks to research methods that make use of involvement, action, and forms of dialogue and social cooperation that are in opposition to the ideal of impersonal observation and experimentation. This position condemns the oppression and hypocrisy of contemporary patriarchal culture but leans towards participation and the key problems faced by women in society, culture, and – above all – science. In management science, the theses of this position were adopted by the critical paradigm.
3 Postmodernist feminism – the least homogeneous, although common epistemological elements include programme inconsistency, a lack of trust in science, subjectivism, and cognitive relativism. Here, there is no objective way of conducting discourse, the perspective of women in lacking. Cognitive relativism enables a move away from the correspondence theory of truth in favour of social epistemology. Numerous interpretations of reality become equal. This position deprives many social disciplines of scientific aspirations, accusing them of ideological entanglement and apparent objectivity. It assumes the rejection of the metanarrative according to the proposal by Lyotard and the unmasking of the myth of masculinist and imperialist science. Feminist discourse makes use of local texts that make sense in a given cultural context, devoid of universal and scientific claims. Postmodernist social sciences are on the boundary of art, social action, and writing, developing the threads of self-irony, symbolic violence, and deconstruction (Haraway 1990).

It is therefore difficult to speak of one paradigm of radical feminism or of a universal feminist theory (see: Lennon 2004, pp. 1013–1024). However, common epistemological assumptions can be identified:

- The pursuit of the development of feminist science, emphasizing women's issues in science;
- Change to the social structure and culture (in a feminist direction);
- Transformation of culturally imposed gender identity;
- Social critique from the perspective of the phenomenon of discrimination against women.

Radical feminism in management consists of critical analysis of theories and practices and of suggesting methods for the emancipation of women, who constitute a discriminated social group. Unmasking the state of inequality and power in the organization and other social structures serves deconstructivism, discursive and narrative analysis, dramaturgical metaphors, and *action research.*

Feminist postmodernism can be used in deconstructivist techniques using the concept of textualism proposed by Derrida (poststructuralism). Content is searched for in the text that comes from the author's subconsciousness or that is the reflection of the cultural context and power. Here we cite the article by Calás and Smircich analysing the text by Mintzberg *The Nature of Managerial Work.* The authors carry out a critique of Mintzberg's masculinist model of leadership, which not only sanctions male power but also allows obsessions of sexual domination to come to the fore (Calás, Smircich 1991, pp. 567–502). H. Mintzberg claimed that Calás and Smircich interpret his text tendentiously, looking for subtexts which are not there. Apparently, hidden patriarchal references can be found in every text – deconstructivism seems to be resistant to reality (Mintzberg 1991, p. 602). It is hard not to agree with the researcher here, deconstruction is based on free interpretation of a text – what counts is not the text itself but the assumed ambiguous subtexts, symbols, associations, and metaphors. When interpreting literary texts, one can refer to subtexts and symbols whose existence the author is aware of or move towards open readings of the work. Organizational activities are not determined solely by rational premises but also by hidden emotions, values, norms, stereotypes, and cultural points of reference. Interpretation of a text involves an attempt to seek a balance between the literal reading of the text and its contextual understanding. We are therefore dealing with a creative process that is at risk of overinterpretation.

The perception of management as an ideology sanctioning the exercising of power is present in the entire critical trend (CMS), which also analyses the management process from the point of view of radical feminism (Ashcraft 2016, pp. 93–106). One subject of criticism is the creation of the manager's social self. The feminist movement unmasks the described elements of its identity. Methods of action should be such unmasking and the implementation of emancipating project methods taking the form of engaged methods, as a part of which the researcher has an emotional relationship with social reality and works on introducing emancipating changes during their research (Brewis, Wray-Bliss 2008, pp. 1521–1540). Research leads to awakening awareness and involvement in social change for discriminated minorities (women, disadvantaged ethnic or sexual groups). Minorities are subject to emancipating actions in the linguistic and pragmatic fields. Here we can cite the example of LGBT, a term which defines a sexual minority and is considered to be politically correct. In this case – according to the principle of *empowerment*, which means giving representatives of a discriminated group, located at the bottom of the social ladder, control over important decisions – the term was transferred from the language of discriminated minorities into general language. Management, sociology, and pedagogics are increasingly open to projects aimed at increasing the proportion of women in power structures as well as in social and political life.

Feminist theories of organizational and social communication present the discrimination of women that reveals itself in language, rhetoric, the separation of public and private discourse, and the exclusion of women from public life (Harris 2016, pp. 150–170). Wood suggests developing communication strategies based on the rhetoric of invitation or changes to masculinist language (Wood 1997, pp. 250–259). Kramarae, referring to Ardner's concept of the 'muted group', is of the opinion that the dominating male linguistic code depreciates and stigmatizes women (Kramarae 1981, pp. 1–63). A solution would be the popularization of a feminist dictionary discussing social experiences from a woman's perspective.

The practical effect of the development of this perspective is emphasizing the negative experiences of women in organizations perpetuating the dominating power structure. Such experiences can include, for example, sexual harassment and mobbing, which have huge psychological consequences, as well as an indirect social and organizational impact (Einarsen 1999, pp. 16–27).

Radical feminism seems to address many social science issues (Gherardi 2003). Organization and management researchers who make use of the concept of radical feminism include Pringle, Burrell, Smircich, Calás, and Czarniawska (Pringle 2005, pp. 284–303). However, the organizational problems of radical feminism seem to be of an interdisciplinary nature and can be analysed from an organizational, sociological, philosophical, and psychological perspective. Here, we can distinguish:

- Research into communication processes and their relationships with masculinist structures (J.T. Wood, Ch. Kramarae);
- The postmodernist reflections of G.C. Spivak, J. Brewis, and J. Butler;
- Problems of the epistemology of feminism and critique of the theory of rational choice;
- Feminist organizational discourse (Gherardi 2003).

The use of radical feminism in management requires in my opinion the indication in every case of the usefulness of such a transgression. To sum up, several implications of the use of radical feminism in management science can be indicated:

- Drawing attention to discriminated social groups;
- Creating new types of social role models based on social sensitivity (a new vision of leadership, human resources management, and the impact of feminist values on identity, organizational culture, and image);
- The possibility to use deconstruction or discursive analysis in the sphere of methodology;

- Undertaking critical analysis of management practice and its achievements (whose continuation takes place within *Critical Management Studies*);
- Emphasizing women's issues, physical and symbolic violence (it is feminists who contributed to unmasking mobbing and sexual harassment in organizations).

What limitations does radical feminism have? These most certainly include inconsistency and the providing of conflicting visions of social and organizational reality. Due to the impossibility of creating even a quasi-paradigm for radical feminism, we can speak mainly of individual concepts and models. Researchers are often afraid of radicalism and the tendentiousness of feminist concepts, as well as their ideological undertones. Additionally, neo-Marxism is inspired by compromised communist thinking and the postmodernist trend by controversial French poststructuralism (Sokal 1996). Evolutionary psychology and neo-Darwinism see in feminism the dogmatic assumption of the cultural dimension of gender and the unprecedented pursuit of gender equality. In spite of everything, gender is not only a cultural construct, although biological, mental and emotional differences cannot of course lead to discrimination in any area of social life (Pinker 2004).

Management has adopted some concepts and methods from radical feminism, however without prior adoption of feminist epistemology as a whole. Drawing attention to the problems of sexual harassment, as well as combatting them thanks to methods of organizational anthropology and discursive analysis, does not equate with acceptance of neo-Marxism or postmodernism. If we are then to talk of adapting feminist epistemology for the needs of empirical research into management, it will correspond most closely to feminist empiricism.

8 Critical View of Paradigm Shifts

From sociological and philosophical sources comes the radical critique of management, that is *Critical Management Studies (CMS)*. The critical trend proposes a move away from relationships of domination and symbolic violence in people's actions both within the organization and in society. We can therefore look for a common point of reference between CMS and HRM (human resource management) in the vision of the individual in the organization; however, the critical trend views this slightly differently. The critique of HRM from the perspective of CMS can be encapsulated in three main threads:

1 The ideology of managerial discourse;
2 The dehumanization of the individual in the organization;
3 The pseudoscience of HRM.

Ideological managerialism, which rationalizes unethical managerial actions and also shapes the identity of the manager and the employee, is based on the 'false consciousness' generated by HRM (Jacques 1996). Representatives of CMS think that HRM can be a dangerous ideology as it possesses tools that make it possible to put theories into practice that agree with inequality and exploitation as well as discrimination of people in organizations under the guise of the natural order. Managers are convinced that their ethics consist of exploiting people's work in order to bring profits to company owners. Personal strategies create managers' identity as exercising power over others and also subordinate to the goals of the organization. The selection of employees is the beginning of their indoctrination; promotion and pay rises constitute rewards for conformism, while employee development must bring benefits to the organization (Alvesson, Willmott 1992, pp. 432–464).

The instrumentalization and dehumanization of HRM are a consequence of the treatment of individuals as a 'resource' or 'capital'. HRM is one of the more influential discourses on management, whether among academics or practitioners. Some researchers of the critical trend believe that the very concept of 'human resources' emphasizes subjectivity, which weighs on the development

DOI: 10.4324/9781003530947-11

of the entire trend, treating people unidimensionally – as a 'resource' that should be rationally allocated and that serves to achieve profits. This is an uncompromising approach in which there is no balancing of the values and interests of the organization with human values, but instead we have dehumanization, as the effect is the exploitation of the individual. The organizations that win are those which are better at indoctrinating and exploiting employees. Managers have a tendency to focus only on work efficiency and competition. Personal strategy and planning the flow of human resources are effective when they maximize profits. Loss of employment and lack of self-realization are secondary problems, consequences of increasing competitiveness that necessitates the use of *reengineering*, *job sharing*, *outsourcing*, etc. There is a spread of 'managerial cynicism', which rewards the effectiveness of managers in exploiting employees. Personal strategy sometimes assumes two different orientations towards two types of employee, which contributes to deepening inequality. Employees with low qualifications and manual employees operate on the employer's market and are often deprived of the possibility for development and self-realization. Meanwhile, managers and specialists at a higher level are treated in accordance with the rules of the employee's market and thus deserve a generous system of remuneration as well as having opportunities for self-realization or even participation in the ownership structure, which merely perpetuates the position of the dominant group.

Exploitation has existed in the organization at every stage of its historical development; with globalization merely bringing a change in dehumanizing practices. Organizational bad practices include not only mobbing and sexual harassment but also bullying and other forms of violence. More disturbing is the spread of these repressive practices, which are not only allowed but even considered competitive: hidden forms of exercising control exploiting symbolic violence, creating fear, and leading to subordination. Personnel management theories do not dedicate much space to contemporary resource management practices of an exploitative nature. Let us give seven examples of these types of practices most frequently encountered in organizations:

1 'Profit before people' – companies focus their activities on profit and not on a social mission

   In the face of increasing competition, the social mission of organizations turns out to be merely window-dressing. Caring for employees is less important than efficiency and profit. Social benefits are restricted, the labour code is broken, or its provisions avoided, and there is no revealing of symptoms of discrimination at all. Trade unions serve mainly a political function, and the defence of employees' interests weakens. Even in organizations with social functions, an attitude of economic efficiency dominates. Healthcare and education place an emphasis on economy, with the availability and quality of services suffering as a result.

2 'Social irresponsibility of the organization' – lack of care for weaker stakeholders

In enterprises, we often see exploitative strategies used with regard to stakeholders and the surroundings, that is a lack of care for employees, the natural environment, and the local community, as well as the spoiling of social capital due to corruption or excessive exploitation of public goods. Entrepreneurs rationalize these actions as practices that are forced upon them by competition and the existing system. Socially irresponsible practices are camouflaged or hidden by *public relations* activities.

3 'Excessive exploitation of employees' – leading to consequences in the form of workaholism

Ever more subtle HRM techniques (such as *job sharing*, *lean management*, or techniques of remuneration based on effectiveness) encourage employees to overexert themselves just to achieve greater work efficiency. Sophisticated forms of information and electronic control in the form of telephone tracking and computer supervision of working time create an 'organizational panopticon' (De Moya, Pallud 2020, pp. 940–976). Employees agree with the conditions imposed on them so as not to lose their jobs, with the consequence being workaholism, which has a very negative impact on their life.

4 'Excessive competition between employees' – promotion is available to employees who act unethically, and there is a lack of cooperation and employee solidarity

An excessive degree of competition between employees is the consequence of the pursuit of professional success at any cost and is linked to how systems and organizational structures are constructed. Cooperative aspects lose out against competitive ones. From being an intermediary and a negotiator working for the interests of employees with regard to the organization, the manager becomes a supervisor focused on task achievement. Concern about the enterprise's competitive position, also within the organization, contribute to higher employee stress levels, as a weakening of the market position may result in redundancies.

5 'Unethical internal marketing' – the effect of promotion on organization members

Marketing messages and promotion take on a manipulative character. On the one hand, we have the creation of the media image of the enterprise, while on the other the instrumentality of goals (market participation, profit, product profitability). Social and legal controls over advertising are ineffective. The creators of advertising sometimes carry out miracles to circumvent legal restrictions, so the effect is the opposite to that intended. Good advertising is in the interest of large producers and the media and as a result ever more frequently fulfils not only an informational role but also a persuasive role based on social engineering and psychomanipulation. Particularly dangerous for an individual's privacy and dignity are rapidly developing forms of internet promotion, which – thanks to algorithms and AI – use a considerable amount of data to identify potential clients. This is also visible in the field of HRM, in which the employee is subjected to propaganda. Recognizing this fact, they are faced with a conflict of values.

6 'The primacy of ownership power' – the owner has priority over other stakeholders

The interests of the owner often overshadow the interests of organizational members, especially in Poland. Morgan gives the limitations of the effectiveness of owner management. Excessive dominance of owners can have a detrimental effect both on the efficiency of the organization and on the employee relations, irrespective of the size of the enterprise.

7 'Anti-participation' – authoritarianism is the most effective

In the face of the transformations currently affecting many sectors, authoritarian managers quickly implement the necessary changes and often prove to be the most effective. This type of management is especially valued in countries with large power distance. Employee participation in management is sometimes considered to be a sign of weakness. More important than employee motivation are procedures for controlling them.

The examples of the dehumanization of HRM described above constitute a worrying vision of an organization in which unethical behaviours occur. Enterprises in the best competitive position strive exclusively for profit, using manipulation and limiting the freedom and creativity of employees. The primacy of economic efficiency may lead to an exploitative enterprise model in which only the interests of the owners or management count. This is an example of an authoritarian and oligarchic vision of economic life – ideas of employee participation and social responsibility are merely propaganda. Operating on the market, in practical terms using mechanisms devoid of competitive ethics, becomes a binary game in which the winner receives all. This way of approaching competition may eliminate the effect of 'socially useful economic egoism' and cause a reduction in social capital.

CMS carried out a radical critique of HRM, which may raise objections in the face of the considerable achievements of this subdiscipline. The critical trend, following neo-Marxism, would seem to reject the foundations of the market economy. However, as an alternative has not yet been found that allows for the development of activity on a large scale, it is hard to agree with the argumentation of radical representatives of CMS. The moderate trend, meanwhile, draws attention to emancipating organizational practices, which are appearing with increasing frequency in countries with free market economies (e.g. Sweden and Denmark). Is a critical perspective on the ideology of managerialism and relationships of dominance in the enterprise at all necessary? Of course, it does not have to be associated with the deconstruction of HRM, but only with a critical view of the relationship between ideology and power.

Representatives of CMS often do not register the fact that the significance of the problems of humanization in HRM is growing. We can, of course, note the instrumental treatment of workers by Taylor. However, Mayo and later Drucker discuss the problems of the individual's emotionality and subjectivity from the point of view of the effectiveness of organizational actions. In HRM, there is a visible evolution from the instrumentalist administration of personnel to talent management and human capital. The critical trend focuses attention on exploitative practices, disregarding the issue of individuals' self-fulfilment and creativity in organizations. For this reason, *CMS* propose a one-dimensional and 'black' vision of the organization, avoiding shades of grey. Of course, there is no lack of organizations of an oppressive nature, but participatory structures are also appearing in enterprises, as well as sustainable remuneration systems, along with the possibility for self-fulfilment. These are examples of the 'humanizing' tendency in organizational practices, which naturally does not mean that the critical view is unnecessary.

CMS mainly puts forward critical proposals with regard to the dominating HRM trend – the number of postulated changes is limited. Management methods (*empowerment*, *parity*) as well as research methods (*action research*, the sociology of intervention, critical discourse analysis) may prove to be useful, but the achievements of CMS on this matter do not equal those of the classical trend. Less orthodox classical approaches to HRM may be inspired by the emancipating research methods and organizational actions of CMS, without recognizing the questionable theoretical and ideological background.

The critical trend in management assumes a flexible vision of human nature. Although there is inequality, exploitation, and domination in social structures, these can be eliminated from the organization and from society. The evolutionary trend does not agree with the full flexibility of human nature (Pinker 2003), as it has universal features (such as hierarchy, the spontaneous creation of power structures and social stratification) that cannot be completely neutralized.

From the perspective of the critical trend, HRM has been shown in a crooked mirror, which ensures social science researchers a certain distance from their research field. This is the function that CMS can serve in HRM. CMS propose a warped view of management science and managerial practice and were formed on the basis of neo-Marxist and postmodernist thinking and radical feminism; the functioning of the organization is explained through the categories of power, domination, symbolic violence, and false consciousness. Although we are aware of the one-sidedness of this view, it is still good to be sensitive to the problems raised by the critical trend, as discrimination of employees and mobbing are not only examples of organizational toxicity but also practices that are justified in some personal theory concepts. The next issue is the desire among employers to have control over the life of employees (the perfect metaphor here is the Benthamite and Foucauldian Panopticon). The problems in which HRM is entangled do actually require critical analysis. In spite of everything, the critical trend should not constitute the dominating discourse, as it does not indicate ways of implementing emancipating changes but merely offers a demystification of the classical approach to management.

In management, it is not easy to make a division between the critical trend and postmodernism, with many researchers using them alternately. Although researchers of the critical trend have defined the differences between the CMS paradigm and postmodernism, in the case of marketing the division is particularly blurred. For this reason, we will use the terms 'critical trend in marketing', 'postmodernist marketing', and 'postmarketing' in the same meaning.

In marketing management, we obtain a rationalist picture of the organization operating on the market which strives for success by satisfying the needs of clients. The relativistic ideas of postmodernism are also in line with contemporary marketing. For this reason, I suggest looking at the most important assumptions of postmodernist marketing. Which features of postmodernism can be related to marketing? There are ten such areas we can identify:

1 Subjectivism and particularism

We must remember that postmodernism is a subjective and relativistic position; incommensurable cultural and linguistic games can be interpreted exclusively subjectively, and there are no universal patterns of truth and meaning, only the 'fruits' of culture. There is also no universalistic understanding of ideas and social roles. Male and female roles, just like leaders and followers or producers and consumers, are only cultural labels that can be freely shaped in social discourse. Subjectivism and particularism in marketing are linked to the assumption of the cultural flexibility of the consumer, which is shaped in the process of communication. Marketing communication can stimulate a fashion in every social sphere (in clothes, music, food or politics, and behaviour).

In the understanding of CMS, brands and the symbolic meanings created through marketing demonstrate aspects of symbolic violence, as they impose 'communication scripts' and stereotypes on culture, that is ready ways in which to understand social reality, closed to reflection. However, the creators of marketing communication cannot fully control the development of the discourse. In culture, some motifs gain importance while others lose it. The creators of such communication suggest certain patterns to recipients and observe to what degree they are adopted. Of course not always – let us not forget the ephemerality of the consumer and the spontaneous development of identities and cultural patterns.

2 Communication in a network of symbolic meanings

It was C. Geertz who insisted that people are entangled in a network of meanings they themselves have created. Derrida spoke of playing with these meanings (textualism and deconstruction). Wittgenstein claimed that the boundaries of our language delineate the boundaries of our world. Baudillard underlined the separation of the symbol from the referent and the creation of meanings in culture. Products, client needs, and fashion are only creations and later a simulation of reality.

Venkatesh considered that we face an 'economy of signs' of a post-material nature. Clients purchase brands, that is meanings interpreted subjectively, thanks to cultural interpretations. Marketing communication takes place principally in the symbolic world. The increasing role of services in the economy, as well as brands and fashion, is a manifestation of marketing as symbolic communication. Marketing is a production system related to the consumption of socially disseminated symbolic meanings. The modernist economy assumed that economic development is influenced not by symbols and meanings but by measurable factors. Despite this, cultural, variable, and subjective brands have conquered the world. Proof of the development of symbolic marketing can be seen in the importance of fashion, irony, protest, and counterculture in the creation and promotion of brands. Postmodernist advertising is no longer the transfer of information and an effect on clients but a symbol together with its interpretation.

3 Cultural relativism

In adopting a postmodernist position, we must agree to cultural relativism and as a consequence the incommensurability of discourses in various cultures. This complicates communication and contradicts its cybernetic understanding as the transfer of data.

However, postmodernist thinking reaches beyond ethnorelativism. Cultural relativism may suggest that marketing exists in the value system of a given culture in which it was created and cannot be applied to other cultural contexts. Here, marketing constitutes a tool of cultural 'colonization' and even the scientific rationalization of this process. Cultural imperialism, as a consequence of promoting a Western value system through means of communication, serves to impose marketing thinking in various societies. Therefore, it is thanks to the media that the categories of the consumer, brand, and advertising spread in different cultures.

4 Epistemological relativism

For postmodernists, the truth is a result of social mediation and is created to a greater degree than it is found. Cognition is not used to describe reality. The correspondence concept of truth, objectivism, and universal criteria of rationality are also abandoned.

Postmodernist anti-epistemology would seem to be appropriate for marketing, which constitutes a field of social activity that creates market reality. Here, theories and research methods are pragmatic and local. One could at this point recall Venkatesh's thought that marketing has always been postmodernist but that it just did not have this awareness. Brand, company image, orientation or marketing strategy, consumer, and organizational identity are not examples of objective categories but of social consensuses, cultural solutions that contain the historically established values and interests of various parties. Marketing, like science, is an activity based on values, in which truth becomes narrative. The organization, the firm, and the market can be interpreted in many different ways (commonly agreed categories, Wittgenstein's 'language games'). An example of such thinking is the use in action of metaphors, paradoxes, and archetypes.

5 Consumerism

Today, consumption has replaced religion and postmodernist ideology. It is now not only the purchase of material goods but a change in lifestyle – consumption has become a condition of existence. The post-material stage means that consumption itself constitutes an internalized need. Products serve to provide individuals and groups with an identity, which is nevertheless fluid due to the increasing pace of consumption. Consuming products is a core metaphor of post-industrial societies. Every human activity (including art, politics, education, and family life) can be encapsulated in transactional and consumer categories. The entire economic systems of developed countries depend on consumption. Marketing promotes a consumption orientation at the cost of a production orientation, referring to various motivations (consumption as style of life, pattern, patriotism, fashion). Financing and distribution encourage consumption, for example, through the increasingly specialized activity of economic entities, while the credit system stimulates consumers' purchasing power through intensive promotion. Consumerism is the fruit of marketing, ensuring its further development. This feedback is visible in the partner, relational, and social marketing concepts, in ever more sophisticated, participating, and qualitative consumer research methods as well as in participatory promotional tools ('street promoters'). Consumer identity in postmodernist consumerism is ephemeral and fragmentary. Analytical market research tools are being abandoned, as are processes of planning marketing strategies, with the market remaining a 'cultural game'. Maintaining a competitive position is increasingly possible thanks to innovativeness and flexibility, which are conducive to consumer loyalty.

6 Fragmentation of the world and the entity

The postmodernist vision of the world turns out to be eclectic. Full cultural diversity is possible due to the conventionality of the criteria for dividing people and groups. In terms of presenting reality, the metaphor of impressionist, expressionist, and surrealist painting may be of use, not that of naturalist painting. Groups, needs, and discourses find themselves in different worlds, which constitute a collage of various narratives and meanings. There is no one key to cognizing and understanding reality. The world and the human self are fragmented.

In marketing, we find this fragmentation in the increasing segmentation and diversity of products as well as in the deconstruction of identity. Consumers are divided into ever smaller groups and are provided with symbolically different products in order to create the impression of individualization.

Modernist marketing assumed reaching customers with a relatively stable structure of 'self', that is with clear (although not always fully conscious) needs, as well as a consistent system of meanings. Postmodernism talks of destabilized identity, and changing, transient consumer choices that are difficult to place in a fixed needs structure. The postmodernist client allows whims and fashion to come to the fore and changes their decisions and expectations, becoming unpredictable.

7 Hyperreality

Postmodernism assumes the multiplicity of realities and their subjective interpretation. Baudrillard uses the term 'simulacre' to describe the process of forming the world experienced by the individual. Today, 'simulacre' is becoming closer to 'hyperreality' created in artificial virtual worlds.

Research into the media, mass communication, and cyberspace bring us closer to postmodernist ideas of hyperreality. The semiotics of Barthes, as well as research by Hall into the ideological impact of the media, prove that social communication can constitute a production process co-creating a reality of cultural meanings. The embodiment of the ideas of hyperreality is both the influence of the mass media and the emergence of cyberspace. Peppers and Rogers refer to the change in marketing paradigm along with the development of the internet – multi-channel, individualized interactive communication replaced single channel communication. Cyberspace can be compared to physical space, books, and films but nevertheless remains different to everyday reality. To put it postmodernistically, in cyberspace we no longer have wanderers, but individuals immersed in a boundless simulation available in their minds and in the process of communication. This presents us with a new challenge – cybermarketing. We do not only mean the conventional use of entirely new tools of promotion and distribution but a change in the cognitive perspective of the consumer and producer. Instead of a model of mass communication with a target consumer segment, we face the task of communicating with a client with a blurred or camouflaged identity. The ephemerality of hyperreality encourages the use of flexibility in marketing strategies, promotion mix tools, and distribution channels. Today, products and services on the internet have new symbolic meanings. Cyberspace can be called a reflection of the idea of entity fragmentation and the orientation towards consumption. On the one hand we have multiple consumer identities, while on the other we have instant access to information and entertainment, satisfying the whims of the postmodernist client. I agree with Hoffman that the internet is not only 'the most important invention since the development of printing' but also a provocation for change, not just in business but 'relating to the essence of being an individual in society'.

8 Marketing and power

For CMS and postmodernism, power is an important issue. Power circulates and it cannot be possessed, but a network-like organization can use and exercise it. Social groups and individuals operate between its threads, constituting vehicles of power, not merely places where it is exercised. According to M. Foucault, power is related to knowledge, as we create truth by dominating over others. There is no other way to exercise power than by 'producing' truth.

Here we can refer to the ethical problems of marketing. In creating meanings and brands (that is symbolic goods), we commit the 'symbolic violence' used in corporations. Influence over communication channels enables manipulation of meanings in order to achieve economic and political interests. Postmodernist marketing has an ethical sensitivity to various forms of marketing manipulation and reveals the social engineering and psychomanipulative position of modernist marketing.

9 Post-Taylorism and Post-Fordism

Taylorism and Fordism are labels for the industrializing modernization of mass society. This concept is based on the assumptions of mass production with the use of economies of scale, supported by uniform consumption (Peaucelle 2000; Rinehart 2001, pp. 179–195). Taylorism and Fordism were created in the spirit of neopositivism and industrialization. The scientific organization of work was expressed in a deterministic division of work into basic sequences carefully controlled by management. Marketing referred to these theories and proposed planned models of sales, communication, distribution, and pricing activity for enterprises operating in conditions of the mass production of goods. Ideas of marketing strategy, marketing research, and marketing mix reached for deterministic assumptions.

The post-industrial economy caused a rejection in management of the Taylor-Ford model of the organization of work. Analysing the birth of the post-industrial society, Bell noted changes towards an informational approach focused on symbolic activity – services and consumption. These processes contributed to adopting a new postmodernist position in management, known as post-Taylorism or post-Fordism, characterized by an orientation towards knowledge and organizational learning, the decentralization of management and the delegation of responsibility, flexible production and distribution, and the dominance of services in the economy.

This position also means changes in marketing management. The organizations of the future, according to some, are to be networked, decentralized and heterarchical, multicultural, and pluralistic, based on symbolic goods, and often taking the form of network enterprises (Hyötyläinen 2000; Basole et al. 2011, pp. 208–230). Organizations of the information society will operate based on self-managing and flexible work teams. The majority of employees should be involved in marketing activities, not only some units. Employees therefore need multidirectional competences in order to rapidly adapt to changing market demands. Multicultural marketing should take into account linguistic and cultural differences and offer multidimensional, network-based, interactive ties with consumers. This would mean the development of partner and relational marketing adapted to the local cultural context. Recognition of social constructionism and the importance of symbolic goods lead marketers to creating and popularizing meanings that have a chance of being included in cultural discourse. Reality is created by communication. The rise in interactive television, telephony and videophony, and communication via the internet demonstrate the dominance of symbols over material aspects of the world.

Postmodernism is a source of valuable critical analyses in the field of marketing management despite its extreme relativism, unclear terminology, ambiguity and programme inconsistency. It enables the rejection of the narrow, instrumental understanding of marketing in favour of a reflexive and ethically sensitive social discipline. It accurately diagnoses changes in contemporary society, such as the economy of brans, consumerism, and multiculturalism. It leads to epistemological reflections and the abandonment of neopositivist paradigms in management science. For this reason, transferring postmodernist motifs into marketing can be fruitful, on condition that they are treated as critical analyses and not attempts to create a new paradigm. In the future, marketing may deal with postmodernist issues, that is the management of meanings, image and identity, symbolic capital, and also qualitative research into consumption and client behaviours.

To sum up, for CMS researchers, power is the core of all social relations, as well as the source of hierarchy and organizational structure. It often takes on camouflaged forms in organizations and heads in an ideological direction (Fournier, Grey 2000, pp. 7–32). The assumption that key issues for the critical trend include power, hierarchy, and structure means that researchers should work on developing the theory of power. However, the achievements of representatives of this trend are meagre, and authors seem to use make use of a concept apparatus belonging to neo-Marxists, poststructuralists, and postmodernists.

Structure is one of the symptoms of the process of distributing power and knowledge, which is why – alongside NFS – it constitutes a subject of interest for alternative paradigms, mainly CMS and postmodernism. The social power relationship is primary to the management process, inextricably linked to the social group, and present at all levels of social and scientific life. Sociology, history, psychology, law, and economics – all are interested in power. In management, as in the other social sciences, it can be understood as a resource (a symbolic good) or a relation (a social relationship).

The issue of power in the organization leads to problems of definition. We can speak of many levels of control: corporate governance, leadership, and micro-power (Fougère, Skålén 2007; Fleming, Spicer 2014, pp. 237–298). Structure is created and perpetuated in two directions. On the one hand, beginning with the macro level, those in power create it and impose it as an organizational project (formal structure). On the other hand, it exists at the grassroots level as micro-power, a complex network of negotiated and renewed relationships between organization members (informal structure). The structuring process leads to the distribution of power at all levels. Each of these forms of power should be interpreted in relational and resource categories. Power is created and developed as a social and organizational relationship, and people understand it as a resource, with the feeling of possessing it, having it at their disposal, and losing it.

Zieleniewski, speaking of structure, has in mind the totality of relationships between elements or between elements and the whole, which is considered from a specific perspective (Zieleniewski 1976). Similar propositions can be found from authors such as Eco, Hjemselv, Lalande, and Krzyżanowski. U. Eco draws attention to three constituent elements of structure: the whole, parts of the whole, and the relations between the parts. Social structure would therefore constitute the ordered relationships between patterns of social behaviour that create a social system. The problem is to distinguish between structure and system.

I propose a definition of social structure in management as networks of power relations and communication between people that create social wholes, such as an organization or a work team. Of key importance in the analysis of social structure is the concept of structuration. Giddens noted the dual nature of social structures – structure influences people's practices, while these create and reproduce social systems. Structuration is based on not only intentional and conscious actions but also habitual, subconscious, and even unconscious actions. Its manifestation are the channels of the flow of power and information.

In a narrower meaning, structure is defined only in relation to the organization. Bielski speaks of the entirety of relations between its elements – people and material components, features, and properties (the 'anatomy' – the static aspect of the organization) as well as relations between events (the 'physiology' – the dynamic aspect of the organization) (Bielski 1996). Strategor establishes the structure in relation to strategy – as the entirety of functions and relations formally specifying the mission of every organizational unit as well as the principles for cooperation between individual parts of the organization. Individual elements of the structure do not exist independently. We can distinguish the following organizational structures: work stations, organizational units, and organizational teams and departments. The relations between elements of the organization are based on an intentional (more seldom: spontaneous) process of structuration.

Of particular importance is the process of the intentional shaping of formal structure by managers. If network structures are developed with blurred organizational boundaries, one should refrain from defining the structure only within it. Structuration, both intentional and formal and also spontaneous, occurs in market networks in the form of networks of alliances, virtual organizations, strategic business units, and branches.

Contemporary organizations – like other social structures – are integrated by ties of power and communication. Coleman is of the opinion that the concept of social structure should be extended to the relations between organizations, not only between people (Coleman 1974, p. 13). Structuration can therefore constitute a form of power. The existence of permanent and strongly integrated structures often means a lack of flexibility, a limited network of contacts with the surroundings, and a lack of resistance to the pace of changes in the environment. In contemporary management, of importance seem to be flexible, heterarchical, and amorphous organizational networks that quickly adapt to changes in the environment as learning and autopoietic systems. The transition towards a network organization does not involve complete rejection of the idea of an organizational structure but its fluid organization around communication processes – the flow of knowledge.

At this point, the question arises whether the flow of information, knowledge, and values has led to a reduction in the importance of power and whether contemporary organizations and the structure of the connections between them are not actually based on the distribution of power.

We are undoubtedly seeing a rise in the importance of knowledge transfer processes in organizational networks. The learning organization acquires knowledge through relations with other entities in operation. Communication between network nodes is a condition for the development of the learning organization. Researchers believe that network societies no longer have a logic of domination, as entities that possess knowledge are sought after instead of those with power. Knowledge transfer supports partnership and limits domination. Despite this, in network management solutions (such as holding networks and virtual, fractal, and *keiretsu* organizations) issues of exercising power and supervision are not treated marginally. For this reason, power – alongside knowledge – continues to constitute a key element of structure, both internally and between organizations. However, this power is no longer hierarchical and total but dispersed and decentralized. Owners, managers, and trade unions merely number among its components. Power can take a symbolic form and reach for increasingly sophisticated forms of control and influence, as it cannot be accused of overt displays of domination. There are many examples of 'soft' power:

- Cultural domination;
- Power networks;

- 'Symbolic violence';
- The authority of science and knowledge;
- 'Power over discourse and language';
- Control over the flow of information.

In these cases, power and structuration do not consist of using force and 'naked violence' but of control and influence in the economic, social, and cultural spheres. Power takes on subtle forms: persuasion, manipulation, and the pressure of authority (personal, traditional, and also competency-based). However, the power relationship as such, imposing the will of others, remains, albeit in a camouflaged form. Individuals and groups in decentralized networks are not subordinated to one hierarchical centre but dispersed power nodes realizing their own interests. These can take on the relational context of coalitions.

The problem of organizational structures is a fundamental issue for management and overshadows issues hiding behind them related to the processes of the flow of knowledge and power. A formal structure reflects stable, established arrangements of organizational roles connected by power and communication. In the face of the need to make the organization more flexible, the formal structure takes on a changeable and less stable form in the shape of a network. At the same time, there is an increase in the importance of the informal structure– the tissue of social organization and the market. Social structure emerges as part of structuring, that is people's activity to perpetuate and reproduce social relationships based on relations of power and communication. Thanks to structuring, people construct social roles and organizations, constituting the social order. Their permanence remains relative and they are maintained by collective consensus – the belief and default consent of social actors. The structuring process is also linked to changes in the social order under the influence of economic, social, political, and technological factors. The informal structure contains a dynamic arrangement of patterns of action of groups and people, reflecting the flows of power and knowledge. The spontaneous uncontrolled informal structure is playing an ever-greater role in the complex network society, greater than that of the formal structure. The cognitive point of view draws our attention to the weightiness of structuring processes and the links between possessing knowledge and exercising power.

It would seem that linking structuring with the process of distributing organizational power brings creative potential to *CMS*. The critical trend understands organizational structures mainly through the lens of domination and oppressiveness (Fournier, Grey 2000; Alvesson, Hardy, Harley 2008, pp. 13–30). Organizational structure is a static representation of power distribution processes. Elements of both the ideology of managerialism and management science include inequality and the unjust division of power, the expression of which is hierarchy and organizational structure. Managers and employees are socialized and educated to build and accept an unequal distribution of power, which they are to consider as the natural order. There are various forms of power distribution and structuring. Functional, divisional, and also radial and network structures can be oppressive and power-oriented. Emphasizing the transformation of structures from hierarchical to heterarchical in network organizations does not equate with the achievement of the assumptions of the critical trend, i.e. the denaturalization of management ideology and the emancipation of marginalized groups. It can be the reverse – network organizations become a more perfect form of exploiting employees than traditional organizations. This is linked to the existence of a global power network and indoctrination, as well as the exploitation of employees from developing countries, and the neo-imperialist practices of international corporations and the governments of richer states (Hardt, Negri 2001).

Researchers of the critical trend begin by analysing various aspects of strategic management in terms of the aforementioned threads. They view organizational strategy as:

1 A tool of 'symbolic violence' – channelling the actions of people in the organization, setting them on the pursuit of profit, and eliminating the moral sphere from the area of interest of management. Decision-makers can therefore attach importance only to the instrumental goals of the organization imposed by the system and rationalize the lack of attention paid to the problems of individuals;
2 The 'false consciousness' of managers and employees;
3 An ideology of managerialism – creating the 'false consciousness' referred to in the previous point, i.e. employee and managerial identities in which the power relationship becomes visible, constituting a camouflage for the actual order;
4 Based on a 'metanarrative' and a 'language game' – assuming faith in predicting the development of the organization or the market, and effective operation and management, on the principle of self-fulfilling prophecy. Strategic management justifies its importance in our discourse, creating 'stories' about its own greatness;
5 An unethical and instrumental social practice – in critically understood social practices, such as communication activities or manifestations of organizational culture, elements can be found an instrumental approach to people, commercialization, masculinism, etc.;
6 A category of political economy – investigating the relationship between economy and politics. This is more an economics position than a management one, according to which the connection between economics and politics constructs and consolidates the principles of resource allocation, profit-making, and the exploitation of people, reflecting a capitalist social order and power relations (Eagleton-Pierce, Knafo 2020, pp. 763–779).

The above division of ways of understanding organizational strategy in CMS is of course simplified; since as a rule, authors use several ways of understanding strategy simultaneously (Alvesson, Willmott 1996). The common element is always an unmasking and constructivist approach to management strategy.

The critical trend of strategic management stands in opposition to the dominating hyperrational understanding of organizational strategy. It refers to the interpretative-symbolic approach and also to postmodernist, feminist, and neo-Marxist perspectives. The critical theory of strategic management is currently on the margins of management, although it is beginning to gain in importance. In terms of theory, it refers to CMS. As far as practice is concerned, apart from a critical view of unjust practices and building false consciousness, it also leans towards methods serving the emancipation and participation of disadvantaged groups.

However, due to the controversial nature of the trend, I propose analysing it critically on two levels. The first is a general critique of the entire trend on three planes: epistemological, methodological, and praxeological. The second detailed level refers to the use of the critical trend in various subdisciplines and in the face of various management problems.

A general critique of CMS leads to the emergence of several overall problems:

1 The debatable philosophical foundations – neo-Marxism and postmodernism;
2 The incorrect understanding of human nature, leading to utopia;
3 Lack of epistemological and institutional maturity;
4 Methodological superficiality;
5 Pragmatic weakness;
6 The hermetic nature of the discourse.

The critical trend has its root in neo-Marxism and postmodernism and thus reflects the cognitive problems of these philosophies. CMS adopted and modified the Marxist perspective of class struggle. Marxism was compromised in the previous century but nevertheless remained in concepts of the critical trend: in management, sociology, and cultural anthropology. Critique of Marxism in the sciences has been conducted, for example, by the neo-classicist school and the Keynesian school. Marxism, as a result of the fall of real socialism and communist ideas, was pushed to the margins of economics. Postmodernism turned out to be equally problematic, especially as the epistemological basis for the development of social science. Mats Alvesson clearly underlines the differences between postmodernism and CMS, but the trends have much in common, for example, a sceptical view of the development of science, the use of discursive methods, the key role of power in organizations, and their call for moral sensitivity (Koss Hartmann 2014, pp. 611–632; Parker, Parker 2017, pp. 1366–1387).

Common pioneers for both trends are Foucault, Lyotard, and Bauman and, in management, Burrell, Schultz, Hatch and Czarniawska. The scepticism relating to social progress connects neo-Marxism and postmodernism and appears in CMS. Its researchers focus on injustices and violence, often not noticing organizational and social progress and improvement in the conditions of human existence. Representatives of CMS do not want to understand that – while economic differences between countries and social groups may deepen – this is not the result of a fall in income among the poorest, but the rapid rise in the wealth of people with the highest incomes. A similar analysis can be conducted with regard to scientific scepticism. The lack of belief in scientific progress that connects postmodernism and CMS becomes irrational in the face of actual scientific progress, also among the social sciences, which of course develop more slowly than the natural sciences. Science is not axiologically neutral but contributes to the development of humankind. Other CMS concepts (the struggle for domination, symbolic violence, false consciousness) can be criticized just as easily as excessively ideological and exaggerated. Postmodernism, with its assumed cultural and epistemological relativism, is not the basis for the development of science, unless understood as a source of metaphors and inspiration.

CMS attempted to transfer the concept of class struggle to the level of the organization. This attempt could not be successful as it was based on incorrect theories regarding human nature. CMS wanted to eliminate the tendencies that have been present in human nature for millions of years. *Homo sapiens* is not a blank sheet of paper or cultural plasticine that can be shaped freely. The desire to exercise power is natural, although corrected socially, but we are not talking here about complete cultural relativism and the possibility of eliminating competition for power and status, which is built in to human nature and social groups. It also leads to the existence of social and organizational inequalities, additionally linked to prestige and hierarchy. Human nature also manifests itself in a cooperative-competitive orientation. Naturally, there are roots for this: the communication process, differences between the sexes, leadership, and organizational culture. Culture and the process of socialization shape our nature, but they cannot take it over completely. The CMS project is utopian as it is responsible for the radical transformation of organization and management in accordance with social, political, and ethical postulates, however not in accordance with human nature.

CMS currently finds itself in the early stages of development; it has not reached the maturity of a paradigm that has overcome numerous phases of development and upheaval. It needs a critical assessment – from its own perspective and also from other paradigms. It would be worth disseminating its concepts as it remains poorly visible in management science analyses in Poland, both in terms of the number of publications and research projects.

CMS is also affected by methodological problems. Its researchers mainly use qualitative and engaged methods specific to the critical trend. However, the experiences of many projects suggest that reaching for methods such as *empowerment* or *action research* in management is not equal to accepting the assumptions of the critical paradigm. *Empowerment* and the strengthening of the position of disadvantaged groups are practical postulates used by the European Union in assessing projects.

Methodological pluralism places emphasis on research triangulation, the need to combine quantitative, qualitative, neutral, and engaged methods. The next problem is reduced methodological rigour as well as greater freedom in interpreting engaged research. It is also accused of excessive interference, almost manipulation through various methods. Such is the criticism that Tourraine's (1978) sociology of intervention encounters.

CMS is characterized by limited pragmatic effectiveness, and very few significant research projects based on the critical paradigm in management can be identified. Organizational change, leading to greater ethical sensitivity, is conducted in various management science paradigms, not only in CMS. For example, business ethics combines philosophical and business threads. The next example is Corporate Social Responsibility, which strives to sensitize the organization to the needs of society. The importance of the humanistic trend is also increasing at the level of organizational behaviours, emphasizing individuals' subjectivity, self-fulfilment, and creativity in the organization. The implementation of projects that have the ambition to make the organization more ethical does not imply a shift to the CMS paradigm. Of course, it is not only CMS representatives who put forward criticism of the management concept. And inversely, not every critique of management science is part of the critical trend (Johnson, Duberley 2003). To be able to talk about criticism from the perspective of the CMS paradigm, it is necessary to use the intellectual tools of this approach, that is to strive for emancipation of marginalized groups and agree with the denaturalization of management science discourse.

A critical perspective on CMS must be differentiated depending on the problem and the chosen subdiscipline. The critical and postmodernist trend seem to be useful from the perspective of marketing analyses, as they expose the manipulative aspects of marketing. However, CMS researchers do not notice that in marketing, concepts have been formulated that are humanizing and respect subjectivity and ethics, such as partnership marketing, relationship marketing, and social marketing. It is also not easy to separate the issues of postmodernism and CMS in marketing. Moreover, the application of the critical trend to human resources management turns out to be creative, as a result of which the image of the subdiscipline itself is distorted. Less effective would seem to be criticism of strategic management from the perspective of this trend. It is right to reveal managers' rationalization camouflaging unethical practices, but this had already appeared in earlier management concepts, e.g. by Weick (1987). CMS postulates relating to organizational culture seem to be of interest, as they draw attention to the oppressive and ideological effect of values and norms. Other threads successfully developed by CMS relate to ideology, the oppressiveness of problems of organizational power and communication, and business ethics. Somewhat forced and weakly rooted in theory are the proposals of some representatives of the critical trend regarding logistics, management accounting, and quality management (Harney, Dunne 2013, pp. 338–349; Gendron 2018, pp. 1–12). In the literature, we can point to many examples of both successful and unsuccessful applications of CMS.

9 Institutional View of Paradigm Shifts

In the institutional structure of science, of greatest importance are the researcher – who contributes to the development of the discipline –and the academic teacher – who transmits knowledge. In management, there is the additional role of the practitioner. In management, the boundary between consulting and scientific activity is often blurred. Researchers not only implement changes in the organization but also design them, while consultants broaden knowledge on the fundamentals of enterprise operation (Gummson 1991, p. 2).

Today, theoreticians and practitioners have a variety of attitudes and social roles that shape identity (Swennen, Jones, Volman 2010; Lamar, Helm 2017). The above typology makes it possible to indicate researchers' degree of engagement in the organization. Every role can contain both a practical and a theoretical orientation (see Table 9.1). By fulfilling the role of member of the supervisory

Table 9.1 Scientific and consulting roles

Criterion	*Scientific roles*	*Consulting roles*
Identity	Scientist	Manager, member of supervisory boards
Objectives	Gaining knowledge and achieving a scientific position (publications, citations)	Customer satisfaction, good image, shaping market position
Methods	Striving for cognitive effectiveness and obtaining access to the research subject	Striving for pragmatic effectiveness
Research field	Related to research projects	Narrowly defined field of organizational consulting
Perspective	Emphasis on creating theory, practice as support for the process	Practical orientation, theory helps only in implementing practices
Quality	The scientific community assesses the quality of the research	The customers and the market assess the quality of consulting

Source: Own elaboration based on Gummson (1991, p. 172).

DOI: 10.4324/9781003530947-12

board or as a manager, the researcher gains knowledge on the functioning of the enterprise, which can then be used for scientific purposes. This combination of roles allows for the development of knowledge and the organization's learning process.

The scientist can become a researcher, a teacher, a practitioner, and also a 'management guru'. Although the organization remains the subject researched, it is viewed from the perspective characteristic for each of the four above roles. For the researcher, the organization constitutes a subject of cognition, for the teacher it is the transfer of knowledge that counts, and for the practitioner it is proposing changes, while the guru focuses on the process of intuitive cognition, which is supposed to induce changes (Peters 1994). Other criteria that differentiate the scientist's roles in management are an orientation towards cognition or action, the pursuit of knowledge, and their relationship to the collective achievements of management. The researchers make use of the achievements, they care about cognition and probable knowledge, they refer to their own academic environment, and they take care of the scientific ethos. The teacher strives to

Table 9.2 Social roles of scientists in management

Social roles	*Researcher*	*Teacher*	*Practitioner*	*Guru*
Subject of research	The organization as a subject of academic cognition (striving for truth)	The organization as a place for the social transmission of knowledge	The organization as an entity subject to changes	The organization as a subject of intuitive cognition and change
Relationship to the achievements of management	Based on achievements (theorizing)	Popularization	Adaptation of pragmatic methodology	Rejection
The pursuit of certainty	Striving for high probability	Striving to transfer the canon of probable knowledge	Operating in conditions of uncertainty	Suggesting certainty
The opposition of cognition and action	Focus on cognition	Focus on communication	Focus on action	Focus on action
Professional ethos	Scientist and researcher	Academic teacher	Consultant	Shaman, prophet
Audience	Scientific environment	Students	Employees, managers, and clients	Businesspeople-believers

Source: Own elaboration.

popularize achievements using the canon of probable knowledge but focuses on communication activities, not on cognition. They address students and defend the teaching ethos. The practitioner focuses on action, often works in conditions of uncertainty, and only selectively makes use of management methods. They are sometimes identified as a consultant, whose audience consists primarily of an enterprise's managers, employees, and clients (Table 9.2).

Naturally, there is often a combination of roles. The researchers become a teacher, day-to-day they are a practitioner, and they may even show an interest in the position of 'management guru'. The researcher can have a practical orientation towards individual solutions, without the possibility for making generalizations, or may also conduct research that is broad in scope and abstract. Often, they reach for other disciplines and become economists, management anthropologists, or organizational sociologists.

The above analysis allows the assumption to be made that two roles are the most universal in contemporary science: the researcher and the academic teacher. The practitioner is often a manager, although they may also play a non-managerial role in the organization. The critical trend reflects on managers' identity. Monin uses critical text analysis, looking for explanations in business classics relating to managerial identity. She analyses texts by authors such as Drucker, Mintzberg, Taylor, Follet, and Kanter, portraying beliefs deeply rooted in the subconscious about the mission of managerial power, the mission of assisting in the pursuit of a better world (See Table 9.3) (Monin 2004, p. 191).

Analyses of the CMS trend show that managerial identity is shaped by influential representatives of our discourse, including 'management gurus'. However, in science we should focus on critical cognitive reflection. In practice, gurus often distort the understanding of management (Pinnington 2001).

Table 9.3 The manager in management classics – observations by Monin

Idea	*Interpretation*	*Manager's vision*
History	They are not a teacher	Managers do not learn from the experiences of the past
Management theory	They can make mistakes	Managers do not learn from past concepts
Management visions	Leads to a better world	Managers must have faith in a vision of the future and achieve it
Life goals	Material	The goal of the manager is obtaining money
Manager's role	Has a mandate to govern	It is an elite group
Employees	Belong to the organization's resources	Managers should control them
Business identity	National identity	Managers' monoculturalism
Success in business	Success is a moral right	Earning as much as possible is a moral right

Source: Own elaboration based on Monin (2004, p. 191).

Where did the role of the guru in our discipline come from? The causes can be found not only in the subject of management but also in its surroundings. S. Andreski described the problems accompanying the development of the social sciences that influenced the emergence of scientific and cognitive pathologies. Applying his theses to management may allow many mistakes to be avoided. Let us divide the problems into three groups:

Ideology in Management

Management is a social discipline that makes the organization the subject of analyses. It is comprised of people, who thanks to the results modify their behaviour and at the same time the subject of research. The possibility to influence the direction of changes constitutes an important ideological tool – in this way it is possible to manipulate society. This manifests itself in the pressure to conduct some research studies at the expense of others. In management, money is allocated for research that sanctions the existing social order; less often do we hear of research into the rationalization of managerial power, the instrumental treatment of people, symbolic violence, total organization, or manipulation in marketing (Grey 1996, pp. 591–612).

Mass Intellectual Property in Management

With its rising popularity, management must deal with the values of the post-industrial society. The market rules of 'mass intellectual property' have entered management, with the most important being market success and the generation by managers and consulting firms of ideas/works that sell the best. Cognitive values must give way to commercial criteria. In terms of the commercialization of management ideas, attention should be drawn to the problem of the popularization and dissemination of science. The areas of the popularization of science and creation are completely mixed in management. The mass goods market has resulted in real theories being replaced by the generation of simplified ideas. Scientific cognition should not be egalitarian; research results are of a specialist or academic nature and are only simplified and made available at the subsequent stage. In management, science takes on the form of 'mass theoretical products', which thanks to their simplicity and obviousness reach all possible recipients: managers, specialists, and also students and laymen. The production of scientific banality has a negative impact on management's reputation. Critics note the apparently complicated terminology actually based on commonplace categories as well as the disregard for in-depth research (Micklethwait, Wooldridge 2000, pp. 19–20). This allows for the comparison of management to tribal medicine and in terms of social development to *show business*. It is said that excessively close ties with the market and commerce may lead to cognitive pathologies, although complete detachment from the market can end in the same way.

The Smokescreen of Jargon

The possibility for communicative consensus is limited to a large degree by two tendencies, that is the increasing ambiguity of basic concepts and the deepening specialization of terminology in subdisciplines of our discourse. The concepts of organization, managing, organizational culture, and many others are ambiguous and seem to create a 'word family'. Every management subdiscipline uses its own terminology, language that is less and less transparent, leading to the hermetization of discourse. Another linguistic problem is the borrowing of terms from other fields and from daily life, causing a mixing of rhetoric and phraseology. By hiding behind its own jargon, management is becoming more hermetic, with specialist communities closing themselves within their own subdisciplines instead of openly communicating. This can be explained by the popularity of 'management shamans', who attract their followers by using simple language.

The problems of the identity of management science would seem to lead to the social role of researchers of organizational processes. As scientists work on their achievements and projects, climbing to the highest rungs of their academic career, they are embedded in the management environment. Corporate consciousness seems to be high here, but often it is really a 'falsified collective consciousness'. Management researchers are a highly varied group specializing in various areas of organizing, including within the fields of economics, law, politics, sociology, and others. Scientists who identify with management are often representatives of other disciplines, from which they borrow cognitive methods. In management subdisciplines, there is a strong differentiation in organizational life: a personnel management researcher has a completely different cognitive perspective to a marketing or finance specialist. Thus, the different specializations in subdisciplines and the origin of management science in other disciplines result in organization researchers having different identities.

The next source of tension in the analysed identities is the previously mentioned dichotomy: management theory (with a predominance of cognitive methods in order to generalize management processes) – management practice (with a predominance of pragmatic methods and the desire to improve the enterprise). Theorists usually belong to the social science academic community, but not only management science, while practitioners are managers and specialists in organizations. The differences manifest themselves in the ways of conducting discourse, the recipients, and the cognitive ideals.

The next problem is the vision of the researcher and management in different cultural environments. The most powerful centre for the development of management is the United States. Another vision of the researcher, and thus methodologies, has taken root in Germany and France. Culturally distinct management concepts have also emerged in Japan, China, and Korea (Lee 2012). While cultural relativism does appear in all social sciences, it does not work to the benefit of the coherence of management science from an international perspective.

The fourth issue is that discussed earlier of the lack of a single management paradigm or even an agreed way of organizing its cognitive perspectives and conflicting images of organizational life. The critical trend proposes something completely different from the functionalists (Koontz 1961).

The fifth reason for a weak researcher identity is the blurring of management science as a subject. Researchers operate in an interdisciplinary manner and work in various research fields. A personnel management researcher needs to know about not only management but also issues of social psychology; a researcher into financial markets is a micro-economist but must also take into account social and macroeconomic variables of the functioning of the economy. A researcher's identity is therefore often assigned to the field they work in rather than the scientific discipline.

To sum up, the unclear identity of the management science researcher has historical and epistemological origins. This has not prevented the development of the science and has ensured considerable reflection, self-criticism, and openness to inspiration. However, there are also negative sides to this phenomenon, which include the strengthening of centrifugal tendencies and the threat of disintegration of the discipline.

Part III

A Practical New Approach to Paradigms in Management Science

10 A New Approach to Creating Knowledge in Management Science

At present, management science is pluralistic in nature. Some researchers see the beginnings of management theory in economics, others reach for its humanistic and social aspects, while still others look to pragmatism in accordance with the rules of the technical sciences. This determines the setting of further cognitive challenges, mainly consisting of critical reference to existing research. There are also fears of the disintegration or marginalization of the discipline.

The cognitive challenges in management science can be organized according to various criteria – as the possibility for practical application of research results, or the value or recognition of scientific achievements. Let us adopt a criterion related to epistemology, that is management science identity. This allows for the identification of five cognitive challenges:

- Management theory and practice;
- The status of scientific theory;
- The multi-paradigm and multi-method nature of management;
- The criterion of scientific value;
- The disintegration of management science.

The first challenge illustrates the tension between theory and practice. Pragmatism places management among the practical sciences, in which usefulness constitutes a significant criterion of scientific value. Theory and practice increasingly head in different directions (Maylor, Turner 2017; Martinez, Peattie, Vazquez-Brust 2021). Theory belongs to academic activity, which focuses on achievements, that is publication in prestigious, highly rated scientific journals, while practical achievements are less highly valued. With its deepening specialization, management science is becoming more hermetic, that is it uses language, concepts, and value systems that may be hard to explain to practitioners not involved in academic work. Researchers of management science most often display popularizing ambitions. That is how we see the role of disseminating science – the aim is to present the more important research results and to select concepts that can be used in organizations and become rooted in

DOI: 10.4324/9781003530947-14

society. At the same time, it is sometimes difficult to determine the boundary between the popularization and trivialization, or even vulgarization, of science. In other words, between presenting the essence of a given theory and distorting its results. It would appear that some management publications aimed at practitioners at times cross this boundary. A multitude of popular publications have appeared on the market that have nothing to do with the reliable transmission of knowledge. The authors – self-styled 'management gurus' – are interested exclusively on promoting themselves. They are in no way similar to such authorities as Peter Drucker, Philip Kotler, Michael Porter, and Igor Ansoff, who were able to describe difficult ideas in simple language. Between the business sector and business schools comes the consulting sector, which only makes use of academic knowledge to a limited degree. In promoting their own concepts for marketing purposes, they avoid subjecting them to any criticism, which contributes to diminishing the authority of management science.

The second cognitive challenge is related to the status of theory in management science. Theory is essential for science, and progress in knowledge does not occur without basic research and scientific generalizations at a higher level. The theories created are applied to the organization. It must only be decided whether it is to be a basic theory or maybe a middle- or short-range theory (Abner, Kim, Perry 2017, pp. 139–159). Basic theories are verified scientific generalizations, thanks to which it is possible to explain a certain area of reality belonging to one or more scientific disciplines. The theory of evolution or quantum mechanics extend beyond one scientific discipline. In the social sciences, it is hard to point to theories with a comparable reach. The interdisciplinary 'systems theory' that drew on the biological sciences seemed to fulfil these conditions. Ackoff and others applied the systems approach to the organization, which enabled the discovery of important features – such as the emergence and interdependence of subsystems and the subsequent creation of systems models. However, there was no possibility of falsification, no criteria for determining that a concept is false. Thus, if we apply Popper's criterion, the cognitive status of systems theory in management becomes similar to the status of psychoanalysis in psychology. For me, such models of the organization are more metaphors than theories as they illustrate and highlight certain processes occurring in the organization. The systems theory of the organization does not address the postulates of the correspondence concept of truth and has probably approached the limits of its possibilities due to the overexploitation of metaphors and the rejection of the scientistic myth of the explanatory power of the world of the organization. Many researchers agree with this, although some include trends such as the interpretative-symbolic approach or even the postmodernist approach in systems theory. The systems theory of the organization shows us how difficult it is to create a universal theory in management science. Some researchers place the science in the group of idiographic sciences that describe and explain reality, but without developing laws as in the nomothetic sciences (natural science).

Knowledge in management science can be non-universal, uncertain, historically determined, and with little 'predictive power', which increases our reserve with regard to the possibility of developing a 'grand theory'. The social sciences avoid being too categorical, and they are historical and situational and operate at a low level of generalization. This may be due to the degree of complexity of the organization, which complicates placing it in a certain framework. It can be assumed that the social sciences have not yet matured to the level of complexity of what they are trying to research. However, there are no significant differences between the world of nature and the social world as a subject of research. Accepting the option of the lack of a universal theory of the organization clearly binds us to ontological dualism. Already in the times of Plato and Descartes, the material and spiritual world were separated and their differences emphasized. Tönnies, Dilthey, and Weber proclaimed the development of the humanities based on their own methods, in contrast to the scientific method of natural science.

Of course, monists and naturalists also came to the fore, recognizing that the foundations of nature and organizational reality were identical. 'Materialism' in physics ceased to be of importance after the relativistic and quantum breakthrough. The monists believed that the phenomena of nature and society also included aspects of the world of information, which were governed by their own laws. However, if theories are formulated, they can be helpful in explaining processes belonging to various sciences. Let us take as an example the 'general theory of replication', according to which entities that wish to self-replicate are created – their carrier can be physical (genes) or informational ('memes'). Dawkins' project has not yet achieved the status of a theory but in the future may fulfil the criterion of falsifiability. If such a theory appears in the world of the organization, it could explain many issues related to marketing, human resource management (HRM), and organizational culture. Thus, at the current stage of social science development, we consider the debate between dualists and monists to be unresolved.

Let us reach now for medium-range theory in the Mertonian sense. In management science, certain generalization can be applied to the organization, of course historically determined and uncertain. They can however be applied (using stochastic categories) or transformed into 'short-range theories', allowing for their practical use to an even more limited degree. Among such examples we find the population ecology of Aldrich, Hannan, and Frejman and the competitive strategies of Porter. The term 'short-range theories' can be applied to conventional cognitive models with a small degree of generalization that facilitate the understanding of organizational processes, such as HRM concepts (the sita model and human capital), marketing (segmentation, targeting, and marketing-mix), and quality management (TQM, kanban).

The above division into 'short-, medium-, and wide-range' theories according to the criterion of the degree of generalization is conventional in nature.

However, if it is not possible today to create a more general theory, maybe it is worth reaching for generalization at a lower level, as social science paradigms are trying to do. If not – we confirm the status of a science offering individual organizational studies, based on the model of cultural studies in the humanities, often devoid of the conventions of scientific discourse.

The third cognitive challenge for management science is its multi-paradigm and multi-method in nature. Many researchers confirm that management does not have its own research methodology but merely uses methods from other disciplines. This is not of course a reason to negate the scientific status of the discipline – the subject of research (the organization) can be understood thanks to research methods from the social sciences or the empirical sciences in general. The multiplicity of management methods is related to the existence of different scientific schools and paradigms as well as the diversity of management subdisciplines (Tronvoll et al. 2011, pp. 560–585). The dominating trend in management relates to neopositivist methods of a quantitative and representative nature: surveys, statistics, para-experiments, and simulations. Alternative paradigms (interpretative-symbolic, critical) prefer qualitative methods with exploratory aspects. The interpretivists reach for the methods of humanistic sociology or organizational anthropology, such as in-depth interviews and discourse analysis (Howcroft, Trauth 2005). The critical trend prefers emancipatory methods that fight the social order based on the division of power (*empowerment*, critical text analysis, etc.). Many authors underline the need to combine methods between paradigms.

Another division of research methods is related to subdisciplines. Marketing, HRM, accounting, and quality management have different goals and use varying tools and techniques. This is due to the fact that differentiation based both on paradigms and subdisciplines gives rise to contradicting research results. If it leads to research triangulation, we can confirm the value of multiple methods, but this is not possible when research results based on various perspectives cannot be harmonized.

The only solution to this problem would be 'methodological eclecticism', meaning the multiplicity of methods or the combination of various perspectives (the meta-paradigmatic approach). In 'epistemological eclecticism', as in pluralism, theories and methods from various paradigms are intertwined. The difference lies only in the relation to research results. Eclecticism allows for contradictions in research results and an inconsistent and non-uniform picture of organization or management which emerges from them. This may also be a result that makes generalization completely impossible.

Organizational and management methodology has ontological and epistemological roots. Understanding both the organization and the management process lies at the foundation of its ontology. Meanwhile, we discover epistemology through cognitive assumptions, which however change along with the development of management as a science. At the beginning it was about developing a 'scientific method', a method that enabled hypotheses to be posed and verified, conclusions to be drawn, and the creation of theory on the basis of empirical research. The ideals of neopositivism and natural science were used in the search for such a method. In the end, use was made of epistemological pluralism – thanks to the insight provided by the social and humanistic sciences and philosophy. Management processes began to be viewed reflexively, using interpretative and constructivist perspectives. The result was the popularization of qualitative research methods, management archetypes, metaphors, and paradoxes. An extreme cognitive approach accepted in management in the 1980s and currently in retreat in the social sciences is postmodernism, according to which management is characterized by conventionalism, relativism, and social constructivism, along with negation of the importance of the correspondence concept of truth.

Management methodology and methods are drawn from the epistemological level, wherein the task of the former is to assess methods' cognitive and pragmatic effectiveness, while the latter constitutes a set of methodologically appropriate rules thanks to which management problems are resolved. Methodology deals with understanding the organization and also its changes. It is hard to define a clear boundary between the practical and cognitive fields. Cognition, as in other social sciences, most often leads to interference in the existing state and results in organizational changes. And vice versa, forming an organization is not devoid of cognitive aspects, and in making changes it is possible to achieve a thorough understanding of the modified organization. Despite this, it is possible to distinguish methods into cognitive and pragmatic – that is practical methods directed towards qualitative change in the organization and the way it is managed.

Analysing the cognitive aspects of scientific methodology already has a long epistemological history. Along with the postulates of the Vienna Circle, hopes were lost of a single 'scientific method' guaranteeing certain knowledge. Popper looked to falsificationism, which was not to provide certain knowledge but to direct scientific knowledge towards stochastic truth by demonstrating the falsification of untrue theories. A milestone in the development of the philosophy of science turned out to be Kuhn's publication in 1968 entitled *The Structure of Scientific Revolutions*. The concept of paradigms and the lack of continuity in the development of science sanctioned the use of many different methods, thanks to which the divergent characteristics of objects were obtained. Kuhn paved the way for the critical trend in the theory of science. Meanwhile, the epistemological anarchy of Feyerabend completely negated the value of scientific methods. By using the 'anything goes' approach, one can also completely reject the classical methodology of science in its entirety. Similar far-reaching ideas also come from the postmodernist trend and the 'strong programme in the sociology of knowledge'.

How can this search for a 'scientific method' be applied to management – does it mean a complete abandonment of this type of enquiry? Creating a general scientific methodology did not bear fruit; scientific disciplines continue to use various cognitive methods. It would be better to now use methodologies called 'local', dedicated to disciplines at a specific stage of development. Management methodology is also not universal; however, it is a reflection on the forming of management methods, thanks to which the researcher can enter the world of the organization. Such methods have naturally been subject to change; thus, the methodology is also enriched with new methods differing in terms of cognitive and practical effectiveness. The search for further methods is dictated not only by work on increasing the effectiveness of tools or their degree of complexity, it is also influenced by fashion, cognitive illusions, the interests and values of social actors, and ideologies. In management there are four basic types of methods that should be subject to methodological reflection: empirical, pragmatic, understanding, and formal.

Empirical methods aim to discover the truth thanks to experience and create scientific knowledge that reflects reality to the highest possible degree. The truth is discovered primarily through induction, which in Popper's opinion has a limited scope. In management, these methods refer to the methods of natural science (e.g. experiment and observation) as well as to the quantitative methods used in the social sciences.

Pragmatic methods, which are the oldest and of a common-sense nature, are not focused on the truth but on solving problems stemming from the collective work that is part of human existence. They reach into reality, but the fundamental criterion of their value is the implementation of effective changes that contribute to greater effectiveness in the organization. In management, these methods make use of casuistry (law), engineering techniques, and practical managerial experience.

Understanding methods draw on the humanities and philosophy, are essentialist in nature, and are about understanding the 'essence of things'. They are composed of concept, phenomenological, dialectic, and hermeneutic analyses. They can also be found in the empirical sciences, specifically in the qualitative methods of the social sciences, to which the interpretative management trend refers. This makes use of methods of organizational ethnology (such as text analysis, ethnological interview, field observation) as well as other interpretative and cognitive sociological methods (here the social intervention method, ethnomethodology, and the grounded theory method). Formal methods emerged along with the development of the ability to think hypothetically. They include mathematics, statistical and logical methods, and deduction. In management, their repertoire reaches for probabilistic and numerical methods, which has cognitive and practical consequences (e.g. econometric and operational research).

Management methodology therefore includes practical and cognitive goals that may overlap, but which also remain in contradiction to one another. Management that is focused on knowledge operates on the basis of the methodologies of the social and natural sciences, while that focused on practical effects – on the basis of common sense and engineering sciences.

It should be mentioned that management methods contain features of all four types of method. In the forecasting and operational research approach there are elements of cognitive formalized methods (such as mathematization) as well as empirical (reflecting reality) and practical methods (increase in effectiveness and productivity). For this reason, it is not possible to treat them homogeneously and separately. For it to be possible to understand and shape management and organization, an open epistemological and methodological position should be adopted, and the assumption should be that it is necessary to combine various methods and use different theories.

The cognitive value of methods depends on the paradigm we select, and the credibility and effectiveness of such methods are among the most significant methodological problems in management science. Credibility corresponds to accuracy (does the method measure what it should measure) and reliability (the precision of measurement) in sociological and psychological methods. Cognitive effectiveness is important primarily in the practical and applied sciences as well as in pragmatic methods that describe both reality and its transformations. In the neopositivist paradigm, the separation of pragmatic and research methods is clear (here the task of the former is to improve the organization, understood using the latter), while in other paradigms this occurs to a considerably lesser degree, for example, from the critical perspective, research should be engaged and result in change. In postmodernism and the interpretative-symbolic paradigm, there is no distance between the researcher and reality; thus, there is no division into cognitive and pragmatic methods. The characteristics of the researcher include commitment, evaluation, and involvement – the subject of research changes as it progresses.

What can we therefore include in methodology characteristic for management science? Ultimately, it is difficult to accuse management of methodological underdevelopment given that other social sciences also draw on research methodology borrowed from other disciplines. It is similar in the case of management, mainly in the field of understanding the organization, although it also has methods specific to itself, primarily regarding the forming and management of the organization. Social research methods, which come from social psychology, sociology, and anthropology, seem to be ideal for understanding the organization, which after all is the target social group.

The effectiveness of methods is continually subject to critical analysis, especially those emerging from new concepts that constitute a certain passing fashion – while excessive requirements are often placed on such methods. Concepts turn out to be a 'marketing product' that is 'sold' both to researchers and to management practitioners. In spite of this, management methodology would seem to contribute to increasing the efficiency and thus competitiveness of the organization. Management methods are subject to modification, as is the organization. It should be noted that the use of pragmatic methods does not determine the success of the organization, but it does increase the probability of such success.

Contemporary management has abandoned 'methodological fundamentalism', which has a very vigorous approach to the method, in line with the neopositivism of the natural sciences. Currently, it is suggested that many methods be used in understanding and forming the organization. For example, Denzin, the author of the methodological triangulation postulate, recognizes the principle of the need to reach for methods that will verify one another or at least complement one another (Denzin 1970). In order to resolve a key research problem, it is worth looking to methods from various approaches and disciplines, applying 'methodological pluralism'. Followers of 'methodological anarchy' view it differently and assume the possibility of using methods irrespective of their origin (whether from a given science or from life).

Management methods should be reached for with caution, as their heuristic nature stands in the way of algorithmization and limits determinism. It is hard to fully verify the cognitive and pragmatic effectiveness of all methods, and therefore, it is worth applying various techniques, while being aware of the possibility of encountering contradictions. After all, similarly to paradoxes or issues for discussion, they are the natural result of exploratory research, in which open questions are posed.

'Methodological eclecticism', which allows for contradictions between scientific methods, finds itself on the axis between liberal 'methodological anarchy' and epistemologically tolerant 'methodological pluralism'. It should be admitted that researchers most often aim to make use of a single methodological approach, which does not automatically mean the adoption of 'methodological fundamentalism'.

The next challenge to management science is the criteria for assessing its cognitive value. Due to the various philosophies that constitute the basis for paradigms, it is not easy to agree on a way to determine cognitive value, while this is the basic task in interpreting research results or conducting one's own research projects. We then most often use heuristic categories appropriate for a given paradigm. The only universal cognitive categories are integrity and the novelty of the scientific product. The criterion of credibility would seem to be essential, at least in the correspondence theory of truth. For paradigms that assume a coherent or other theory of truth (social constructivism), of greater importance is the criterion of intersubjective consensus or pragmatic effectiveness. My proposal therefore constitutes the adoption in management science of cognitive value criteria in accordance with the applied paradigm. By applying Burrell and G. Morgan's division, we distinguish three paradigms:

- Neopositivist-functionalist-systemic;
- Interpretative-symbolic;
- Critical.

In terms of the neopositivist paradigm, I would propose the scientific value criteria (originating in the natural sciences) of cognitive reliability and credibility, the possibility of falsification or verification, and coherence with research results. In the case of interpretivism, more important are pragmatism and coherence and to a somewhat lesser degree falsificationism. Here, the cognitive value criteria include not only coherence with research results and cognitive credibility but also consensus in the scientific community and effectiveness in forming organizational reality.

In the critical trend, we should mention the criteria: effective disclosure of hidden dependencies between power and oppression as well as implementation of emancipating changes (here we note the consistency with interpretivism), while at the end are cognitive credibility and coherence with research results. Table 10.1 summarizes the criteria,

The fifth challenge to management science are their centrifugal tendencies, leading even to attempts to disintegrate the discipline. The discussed multiplicity of research methodologies and subjects, along with the multiplicity of paradigms and subdisciplines, related of course to pragmatic differentiation, plays a deciding role here. Management problems are found at the boundary of other disciplines, and for this reason the nature of the science is of overlapping but poorly integrated research fields. The identity of the researcher is not precisely defined and belongs to specific fields in given subdisciplines in different schools and paradigms.

Management science could jokingly be said to be a victim of its own success. It has grown hugely in importance due to the popularity of managers – currently

Table 10.1 Cognitive value criteria in three management science paradigms

Criterion	*Paradigm*		
	Neopositivist-functionalist-systemic	*Interpretative-symbolic*	*Critical*
Cognitive credibility	√	√	√
Cognitive reliability	√	X	X
Cognitive validity	√	X	X
Novelty	√	√	√
Possibility of verification or falsification	√	X	X
Effectiveness of forming organizational reality	X	√	√
Effectiveness of disclosing power relations	X	X	√
Coherence with other research results	√	√	√
Integrity in presenting results	√	√	√

Source: Own elaboration (X indicates no criterion).

the largest social group in power. Despite this, it does not have a strong scientific identity or a single theory of the organization and has limited practical applications at its disposal. There has been a fragmentation of schools and paradigms with no synthesis effect. Critical and methodological reflection is therefore needed. Not only should specific problems be researched, but the methods and the role of management science in the contemporary world should also be analysed. Let us treat the challenges as cognitive dilemmas without easy solutions but which nevertheless contribute to the development of management science. An open attitude seems to be the most promising as it invites discussion on theories and methods from different perspectives. However, it should be remembered that the application of methodological pluralism does not free us from the obligation to fulfil assessment criteria regarding the scientific value of research results. The lack of universal criteria does not mean that the quality of scientific creativity ceases to be the most important.

11 Paradigm Shifts in Human Resources Management

Human resource management (HRM) is a part of management science, operates on a meso- and micro-social level, and deals with the individual in the organization. It therefore addresses not only problems of the organization and management (such as organizational culture, HR strategy, and managing) but also sociology (such as identification, power, and communicating), pedagogics (such as education), and social psychology (secondary socialization and motivating) (Thursfield, Hamblett 2004, pp. 113–130). The HRM subdiscipline has a strong professional identity (Peticca-Harris, McKenna 2013). The emergence of this discipline is also connected to challenges of an epistemological and methodological nature, with the question arising of how to classify theories and research methods originating in other disciplines.

In terms of the HR function in organizations, many various proposals for paradigms and typologies can be found in management theory. It seems, however, that a broad and supportive cognitive framework may be the modified proposal of paradigms taken from Burrell and Morgan and widely used in this work (Primecz 2020, pp. 124–147). Typologies of HRM concepts most often refer to its history and practice. Some point to the evolution within the HR function – beginning with the HR administration process and ending with HRM.

Other concepts make a dichotomous opposition between HRM and human capital management. I therefore propose looking at HRM through the lens of social science paradigms and their division by Burrell and Morgan (1979). Smircich notes that this division into paradigms can be applied in order to better understand organizational culture. In my opinion, it is similar in the case of HRM. By using a multi-paradigm approach for the needs of HRM, an insight can be gained into the (very often conflicting) research theories, methods, and tools related to the HR function.

In HRM practice and theory, the NFS paradigm dominates. Theories and methods of recruitment, training, development, motivation, and HR strategy use a functionalist way of thinking. During recruitment, people are sought who have the appropriate competencies (that is the knowledge, skills, and psycho-physical predisposition) suitable for the position that the organization can offer them.

DOI: 10.4324/9781003530947-15

Such competencies must be clearly defined as well as measurable using methods of selection and personal diagnosis. In this approach, there is no real place for intuition, silent knowledge, or adapting to a particular organizational culture or social group, as focused on by alternative paradigms. The role of individual and collective identity is usually omitted. Personnel management traditionally draws on motivational concepts in the form of Maslow's pyramid of needs and Herzberg's needs diagram, as they refer to the instrumental treatment of human nature originating in behaviourism. People shape their behaviours depending on the system of rewards and punishments, and therefore the reason for their actions is the motivation system. Other concepts make the picture of human behaviours more complex; for example, cognitive concepts talk of the psycho-social process of processing stimuli and taking action, from instinctive reactions to conscious decisions. Meanwhile, the psycho-dynamic concept looks for motivation hidden in the subconscious. The same analysis can be conducted in the case of the remaining elements of HRM (that is training, promotion, and planning the development of HR strategy).

Most often, HRM authors and practitioners do not think about the cognitive canon used, for them it is obvious. HRM and the organizational behaviour associated with it have followed a dynamic development path in the United States, where a scientistic variety of empirical psychology dominated, i.e. behaviourism, according to which human actions were interpreted in the categories of stimulus-response couplings, disregarding introspection, emotions, and subjectivity (Lengnick-Hall et al. 2009, pp. 64–85). However, cognitive psychology and humanistic psychology have shown that such assumptions were misplaced. Despite this, 'traces' of behaviourism can still be found in the HRM NFS paradigm. These include:

- The belief in the possibility to shape human nature in the management process;
- Reductionism, which wants to explain the functioning of people in the organization using the analysis of cause-and-effect variables;
- Methodological individualism, which draws attention to individual human reactions, not to socio-cultural factors;
- The preference for quantifiable research and practical methods and techniques;
- The wish to have control over employees' actions in the enterprise;
- Personal systems based on the coupling of stimuli and anticipated reactions;
- Striving for scientism, building theoretical systems, and developing them into a rigorous methodology.

However, the functionalist way of thinking remains helpless in the face of many organizational phenomena. The description of communication processes, leadership, employee development, or organizational identity and culture is criticized for being too slow and oversimplified, which makes it difficult to use.

This is something encountered by practitioners who want to implement 'model' recruitment procedures, evaluation and motivation systems, or tools for changing organizational culture.

The interpretative-symbolic paradigm was absorbed into HRM from other social sciences starting in the 1970s, causing a redefinition of some ideas and concepts in this subdiscipline. Thanks to the paradigm, they have a symbolic, social, and metaphorical dimension and can constitute the subject of various interpretative and collective representations. At this point, we point to interpretative ways of perceiving organizational culture, HR strategy, and leadership.

The NFS paradigm is not concerned with either culture or organizational identity. These concepts emerged in management due to analyses of the effect of collective consciousness and ideas on the organization. In the IS paradigm, culture is often a core metaphor – that is how the process of organizing itself is understood. Organizing is understood primarily as a cognitive undertaking, human forms of expression, symbolic action, and manifestations of deep structures of the mind, including collective consciousness. Interpretivists in HRM analyse such processes as establishing organizational boundaries and shaping meanings and cultural processes. These phenomena mainly occur spontaneously and unprompted, and managerial control remains limited. For these reasons, an important role is played by intuition and collective values and norms, therefore the individualism and reductionism characteristic of NFS no longer count; instead we have holism, social factors, and culturalism. People's feedback in organizations is described by the processes of the management of meanings and sensemaking or sensegiving.

In IS, HR strategy, as an element of the organization's strategy as a whole, has an incremental and emergent dimension and thus is born of action, is variable and evolutionary, and can be rationalized. In the interpretative model, a strategy is perceived through the lens of its formation, experience, and implementation by a social group. A strategy is no longer a rational decision-making process conducted on the basis of reliable knowledge but a social process. Employment, motivation, derecruitment, and employee development are nothing more than the consequences of the social game of stakeholders and managers' experiences of the organizational situation. This model rarely sees strategy as a political process in which there is a clash between interest groups and the formation of coalitions aimed at strengthening power or achieving conflicting interests. The strategic process is no longer strategic in nature, planning interweaves with implementation and control, and changes to the plan can take place at any time during the process. Strategy is created by the action of managers, and planning is a means for rationalizing a future that is hard to predict.

Leadership concepts that use this way of thinking draw attention to the symbolic and social conditions of the function of leader. Leadership does not stem from personal charisma; it is a kind of social bond and image with which members of the group can identify. A leader realizes a certain mission, and elements of leading include emotions, interaction in a group, and communication processes, thanks to which the image of the leader is shaped and developed. Interpretivists see leadership as a process of the management of meanings. The leader should know how to subconsciously persuade the group to adopt his or her interpretation of the organizational situation.

The interpretative trend brought many qualitative methods and research techniques to HRM, including the engaged and participatory methods originating in cultural anthropology. It is worth mentioning here such techniques as the in-depth interview (biographical, anthropological), participatory observation, text analysis, etc. One can also reach for methodologies related to organizational anthropology but rooted in sociology: the sociology of intervention, ethnomethodology, participatory research, grounded theory, and the extended case study method. These methods ensure that the tools have an impact on social processes in organizations. In Poland, interpretivists are interested in issues of social research methodology and management practice and most often address problems such as management roles, social capital, organizational culture and identity, and communication and cooperation in organizations.

The term 'human resource' is in itself a metaphor that instrumentalizes the individual in the organization. The radical structuralism paradigm in HRM consists of critical analysis of the discipline's practices as well as presenting methods for emancipating discriminated social groups. From the perspective of radical structuralism, HRM is used to manipulate organization members, while the theory seems to accept ideologies as objective truths (Fournier, Grey 2000, pp. 7–32).

Critical analysis methods in HRM serve to unmask inequalities and power in organizations using dramaturgical metaphors, discursive analysis, and radical feminist methodology. Researchers of this subdiscipline, who make use of the thinking of the radical structuralism paradigm, include Deetz, Alvesson, Willmott, and others. Radical structuralism in HRM is yet to see methodological development. In Poland, its followers include representatives of radical feminism who address the domination of men in power structures within enterprises.

Postmodernism does not provide methods and tools for HRM (due to its anti-system and anti-method nature) but leads to a critical take on people's behaviours in organizations. It proposes looking at the organization through metaphors, paradoxes, antinomies, and the poetic logic of organizing and addresses above all the problem of the individual with regard to the organization. Burrell, Willmott, Bauman, and others see the causes of the lack of stability and employee trust in the organization in the processes of the fragmentation and virtualization of human labour. Corley, Hatch, Schultz, Gioia, and Czarniawska talk of the impossibility of distinguishing culture from organizational processes and acquiring a dimension of fluid individual and collective identity. Postmodernism also sees problems of sexuality in the workplace. Here it employs an approach reminiscent of radical feminism but enriches with reflection regarding the fragmentation of identity and social diversity. This paradigm also leads to the deconstruction of the Weberian understanding of charismatic leadership as a metanarrative. Other threads analysed include:

- Hyperreality as a work environment;
- The disintegration of human identity in conditions of the consumer society;
- Linking intellectual capital with problems of domination (knowledge-power dialectics);
- The deconstruction of existing HRM concepts (e.g. professional category, career, employee development).

The theories presented above are only an example of the use of thinking from four paradigms are at various stages of development in terms of theory and methodology. Here, functionalism is the most mature as it has its own tools of conceptualization and management. The helplessness of this paradigm with regard to social dilemmas contributed to the development of interpretative-systemic concept methods. Radical structuralism and postmodernism are primarily critical threads of reflection on HRM. One can therefore talk of the dualist development of the subdiscipline: classical and alternative HRM theories. However, we must remember that the latter have different epistemic ideals, despite the fact that they begin from criticism of the dominating functionalist paradigm.

The application in HRM of the four paradigms distinguished in the social sciences brings important consequences for the theory and practice of the subdiscipline. Each paradigm has different cognitive foundations, so criticism of the concept should be conducted from two perspectives: from the same or also another paradigm. The same problem can be looked at from the perspective of different paradigms, which leads to creative though sometimes paradoxical solutions in personnel management. For example, organizational culture from a functionalist perspective can be described in the form of variables, the recognition of which enables control of cultural changes. In the IS paradigm, such control is totally impossible due to the fact that we have spontaneous, indeterministic processes that occur within complex games of actors and social groups. Radical structuralism will make the diagnosis that organizational culture is a tool of domination, control, and power and will strive to weaken its oppressiveness as well as emancipate disadvantaged groups. Among the postmodernists, the concept of organizational culture will be subject to deconstruction and will become a linguistic game and a narrative, a pure emanation of the internal discourse of social disciplines, not rooted in social reality. A similar analysis on the basis of paradigms can be conducted in the case of other fundamental concepts such as structure, communication, power, and values. A proper reading of the message of each of these perspectives enables a better understanding of the phenomena being analysed.

12 Paradigm Shifts in Strategic Management

Strategic management has developed its own management trend typologies. Apart from the classical typologies of Drucker, Porter, Ansoff, Weick, and Mintzberg there are many new interesting classifications in the literature. Other researchers add the schools of entrepreneurship, culture and learning (Sandberg 1992, pp. 73–90). Still others additionally note the cognitive and power trends (Yi, Yongxia 2007). It can therefore be unequivocally stated that there is a multiplicity of classification of trends, paradigms, and strategic management schools and that there is no consensus among researchers as to which convention we should consider as binding.

For this reason, it is possible to make use of strategic management paradigms on the basis of the Burrell and Morgan model but on the following conditions:

1 The division into paradigms does not reflect the complexity of concepts or the process of their historical and institutional formation in scientific schools, which means that the Burrell and Morgan paradigm perspective is one of many possible approaches.
2 The methodological reflection of strategic management has been expanded, with emphasis placed on pluralism, triangulation, and methodological awareness.
3 In strategic management, self-critical analyses are carried out, which prove the internal diversity of both paradigms and cognitive perspectives.
4 Pragmatism is assumed, as the relations between theory and practice are crucial for the development of the subdiscipline due to the roles of decision-makers (Mir, Watson 2000, pp. 941–953).

The Burrell and Morgan paradigm matrix does not reflect the division axis of strategic management theory. Evolutionary and resource concepts of strategy can simultaneously be located in two paradigms. The category of alternative paradigms is not developed. For this reason it is recommended to look for better methods of classifying paradigms in strategic management.

For example, this could be by expanding the Burrell/Morgan proposal by defining the type of rationality on which strategic management theory is based.

DOI: 10.4324/9781003530947-16

We pass from complete rationality, through rationality bounded by access to market information and rationality bounded by the specifics of the human cognitive apparatus (socio-cultural and biological), until we reach complete irrationality.

The planning model, whose followers include classical strategic management authors, is dominated by the assumptions of organizational engineering and *homo oeconomicus*. In this model, the description of planning is encompassed in the categories of complete rationality, with strategy constituting a sequential plan implemented according to the decisions of managers. Strategy is of a 'scientific' nature, i.e. it is based upon objective data as well as algorithmic analysis methods (most often quantitative). The strategic process is linear; after planning we move to implementation and control. Both the planner and the strategist or manager strive to access the greatest amount of information, thanks to which plans and decisions are formed that have the greatest probability of being realized.

The model of bounded rationality, which draws on the concept of Simon (1991), takes into account the consequences of implementing strategy in the planning model. The awareness of the complexity of the organization and its surroundings, as well as the rapid pace of change, forces us to assume bounded rationality (Gazheli, Antal, van den Bergh 2015, pp. 14–30). A strategy is based on available, selected data that are processed using both algorithmic and heuristic methods. The strategic process is no longer linear, and the division between planning, implementation, and control becomes fluid. Managers want to acquire crucial information and, on its basis, develop scenarios and strategy variants. Such thinking is represented, for example, by Mintzberg and Wrapp.

The interpretative model perceives strategy through the lens of its formation and understanding by a social group. Here we have the socio-emotional dimension of strategy, which no longer constitutes a rational decision-making process conducted on the basis of reliable knowledge. Heuristic and interpretative methods are used. In this model, strategy is a political process in which various interest groups clash and where coalitions are created that aim to consolidate power in organizations. Planning merges with implementation, and control takes place in the whole synchronous process. Planning contributes to integrating and motivating employees as well as rationalizing a hard to predict future. Strategy is created in the actions of the manager. Weick's concepts of emergent strategies and Quinn's logical incrementalism are examples of interpretative concepts.

The radical strategy model is related to the development in the social sciences of both the critical trend (the Frankfurt school, radical feminism, and neo-Marxism) and the postmodernist trend (deconstruction, textualism). Strategy aims are devoid of rational elements. The postmodernist strategy is merely a 'smokescreen' obscuring the struggle for power in the group, and there is no option for planning the future. The radical trend in strategic management has not developed an extensive theoretical layer. Its followers cast doubt on the sense of practising this discipline in its current form. Burrell and Clegg adopted a critical position from the point of view of the issue of power. In the radical trend we can distinguish the critical and postmodernist aspect. The critical understanding of strategy is related to its manipulative, oppressive role, and the pursuit of control over employees (Shrivastava 1986, pp. 363–377). Domination and power serve inequalities and an unjust order. The postmodernist understanding of strategy also exposes the oppressiveness of power but above all speaks of the irrationality of decision-making (Hambrick, Chen 2008, pp. 32–54).

It is also worth confronting strategic management paradigms with the way of planning the future. The planning model assumed an objective description and planning in conditions close to certainty. A well-planned strategy should contribute to success in the future. In the bounded rationality model we have the description of probable and also limited access to information as well as the changeability of the surroundings and the complexity of the organization. A strategy may come true, or at least one of its described variants, with a certain probability. The interpretative model uses an intersubjective description, and concepts are shared – or only understood – by group members through communication processes. The strategy does not actually have to come true, its task is to motivate people to take action, to integrate them around set goals, to stimulate entrepreneurship and innovativeness, and to rationalize reality. The radical model assumes an exclusively intersubjective perception of reality and only temporary consensuses. Strategy is a linguistic game and a stylized convention, with no possibility to predict or even plan for the future.

To simplify the cognitive foundations of strategic management, we can use the knowledge-belief dichotomy. We can locate the pole of knowledge in neopositivism, referred to by the orthodox scientistic trend present not only in management but also in sociology, social psychology, and cultural anthropology. The extreme pole of belief is present in the humanistic trend reaching to hermeneutics, which is developing in various social sciences, including in management.

The epistemological theory of strategic management is situated between the above two poles: strategies based only on knowledge (hyperrational) and on belief (hyperemotional). Followers of the former negate the emotional and social aspects of strategy, choosing an over-rationalized vision. This thinking is preferred by management theorists with economic and technical roots, referring to neopositivism. This corresponds to the objectivist, planning strategic management model from the described matrix. Meanwhile, hyperemotivists focus on the unpredictable and uncontrollable social and emotional actions of organizational actors, choosing in turn an over-sociologized vision. They make use of ideas originating mainly in humanistic sociology and cultural anthropology. The hyperemotional strategy is the equivalent of the interpretative model as well as – in some aspects – the radical model (subjectivism). This dichotomy is illustrated in Table 12.1.

The development of a coherent approach to strategy is no mean feat. No extreme position seems to be appropriate as we have the dialectics of knowledge

Table 12.1 Poles of strategy theory

Criterion	*Strategy*	
	Hyperrational	*Hyperemotional*
Understanding of the strategy	Effective implementation of decision-makers' plans through knowledge processing and shaping the organization and its surroundings	The process of social construction of the organization and its interpretation by various social groups as well as groups of actors – with no control over the results
Role of strategic planning	Predictive (predicting the future) Adaptive (adapting the organization's actions to the surroundings). Exercising influence (on the surroundings)	Emotive Perceptive (providing interpretations of reality) Integrative (combining people in teams to realize common goals)
Role of the strategist	Has exclusive knowledge and is responsible for its use for the needs of the organization's goals	Leader, organizational hero motivating people to participate in organizational actions
Strategic entity	Unit Individual	Collective Social
Organization surroundings	Separative – strict separation of the organization from the surroundings (legal, structural)	Integrative – the organization blends in with the surroundings Processual understanding of the organization
Necessary knowledge	Certain or very probable Objective In large amounts	Uncertain Subjective Selective (possible excess of knowledge, which results in 'overinterpretation')
Importance of belief, emotions, intuition	Marginalized Unconscious	Crucial Conscious Expressed
Strategy metaphors	War Game with a limited number of variants	Happening Theatre Arena Open game
Strategic management methods	*Planning* SWOT Sectoral analysis Analysis of strategic groups	*Heuristic* Creative (brainstorm) Psychological (projective) Social (*team building*)
Effects of the applied strategy	Implemented plan Greater knowledge of the organization and the surroundings Objectively described change	Subjectively and intersubjectively perceived change

(*Continued*)

Table 12.1 (Continued)

Criterion	*Strategy*	
	Hyperrational	*Hyperemotional*
Importance of the axiological sphere from the viewpoint of strategy	Marginalized	Crucial
Theorists	Ansoff, Ackoff, Porter	Weick, Morgan, Hatch, Clegg
Analogies to strategy schools	Planning Resource Positioning	Evolutionary Resource (dominated by social, cultural, and intellectual capital)

Source: Own elaboration.

and belief. Both management theorists and practitioners want to take part in a rational, conscious decision-making process (knowledge). However, rationality is conditioned by values, intuition, collective consciousness, and unconscious emotions (belief). For this reason, it seems appropriate to balance the two presented perspectives. In the description of strategy and the planning process, it would be good to combine aspects of rationality (in the sphere of achieving goals and methods of action) with emotional, social, and axiological aspects (games of interest, conflicts, values). The dominating perspective of strategic management fits into the scheme of objectivist science, which is to ensure managers knowledge allowing them to take accurate organizational decisions. The interpretative-symbolic, critical, and postmodernist approaches also present a proposal for understanding strategy.

Strategic management of the dominant trend has several common features. At the foundations of strategy theory in management science lies the assumption of rational decision-making by managers. An idealized image of the rationality of strategy is applied in game theory in management; however, even here extreme rationalist attitudes have not caught on. New inspirations referring to the theory of chaos and complexity constitute non-linear and indeterministic sources of strategic thinking. The social context of the decision-making process shatters the belief in the rationality of strategy. The classical management trend adopted the following guidelines with regard to the issue of shaping strategy:

1 Creating a strategy requires the greatest possible amount of information, which is processed into knowledge;
2 A strategy is a formalized plan of action of a long-term nature;
3 The manager creates and implements a strategy;

4 Strategic decisions are taken rationally;
5 The organization's surroundings are characterized by a considerable degree of predictability.

Doubts regarding these assumptions have been expressed by many representatives of non-functionalist paradigms.

1 Market data are of course necessary for creating a strategy. However, there is no guarantee of obtaining reliable data, nor of a cognitively neutral process of obtaining and interpreting such information. Part of the data is noise; part passes through an interpretative filter and serves only to confirm decisions already taken. An excess of information creates problems with its selection.
2 Effective planning in strategic management should be formalized and long term. Formalized planning is a process based on an algorithm and is not heuristic. It was assumed that the market data obtained (referred to in point 1) enabled the appropriate strategy to be built, which turned out to be unreliable. Strategic analysis methods may help, but heuristic processes constitute the foundation. Managing an organization is also an art that defies deterministic categories. Long-term planning becomes problematic in conditions of significant changeability in the surroundings, as the plan quickly becomes out of date, and rigid attachment to strategic goals may lock the organization into short-term opportunities and mean a lack of flexibility.
3 The organization's actions are here understood as the effect of managerial decisions; therefore, it is considered that the strategist's decisions are fully reflected in the organization's actions. However, other factors also have an impact on the organization's activities, including those outside direct control. Decision-making is not connected to straightforward maximization of profits. People perceive market reality differently; they have different goals, needs, and expectations; and it is therefore difficult to predict their behaviour, especially in the case of the dispersion of power. The struggle for power in the organization and the conflicting interests of various groups complicate the selection of rational strategic options. Strategic decisions are connected to the process of perceiving reality. The cognitive approach tells us that the individual's mind does not reflect reality but carries out a reconstruction depending on their cognitive apparatus. Individual and social experiences therefore have an indirect influence on decision-making. The manager experiences a 'filtered' reality and is entangled in perceptual illusions and stereotypes.
4 Rationality is also not devoid of cultural and the cognitive conditioning. Plans are a game that depends on political coalitions, the emotions and interests of employees, and also meanings and symbols. The organization's strategic goals may vary. It is difficult to rationally assess what will be better: market share, achieving profits, or social responsibility. The choice is made on

the basis of many factors, situational and cognitive conditions, and the value systems of the individual and society.

5 There is no denying organizations' turbulent and unpredictable surroundings, which are subject to the pressure of changes related to globalization; scientific and technical progress; and social, political, and cultural transformation. Assumptions of predetermination lead to utopian strategies, and predicting the status of social, economic, and political variables in conditions of permanent changeability makes no sense.

Criticism of the unrealistic theses of classical planners leads to the question of whether management science can develop without strategy theory. Does strategy without goals and a planning process make any sense? Maybe we should not talk of strategy, but exclusively of goals and other concepts unburdened by theory, or maybe strategies are treated too literally. For example, strategy understood as a metaphor and paradox emphasizes certain aspects but obscures others. The focus on strategy theory is related to ways designed for its understanding and implementation, which have been popularized and applied in practice but which have not brought the expected results. However, the probability that strategy will disappear from the canon of management is minimal. The necessity of developing strategic management can be justified in three ways.

The first argument is pragmatic in nature – managers' thinking is geared towards creating strategy, even if they perceive the weakness of an over-rationalized version of strategic management and know that strategic analysis tools do not guarantee success and that excessive attachment to the mission can result in market opportunities that arise not being exploited. In spite of everything, the concepts and methods of strategic management are rooted for good and management practice. It is hard to talk of taking action, exercising power, and communicating in organizations without strategies, goals, and a mission. For this reason, it is better to modify strategic management theory rather than abandon it entirely.

The second argument is social in nature and concerns the institutional distinctiveness of management science. It is so popular, also because of its strategies, that rejecting a popular research field would seem to be unjustified.

The third argument, in my view the most important, is epistemological in nature. The human cognitive apparatus features teleological, temporal, and predictive thinking, thus for perceiving and interpreting ourselves and our surroundings we use the goal category and a time perspective. Planning is written in to the human mind and contributes to reducing uncertainties. Goals and plans will always be present in some form in the organization's cognition and action. After all, identifying strategy with the process of planning the implementation of goals through management constitutes the epistemological basis of strategic management (Laureiro-Martínez, Brusoni 2018, pp. 1031–1058).

However, this does not mean that we should leave strategy at the service of hyperrationalist thinking. Quite the opposite: I am in favour of developing interpretative approaches in strategic management. So what should they be characterized by?

1 Above all an interpretative process of creating and implementing strategy, consisting of constructing and interpreting organizational reality. The manager is a creator not only a researcher of reality. Weick proposed concepts of emergent strategies, appearing in the course of the organization's actions, and not re-formulated strategies. Another example of the interpretative approach is Quinn's logical incrementalism in creating strategy. Yet another is the critical trend, symbolism, and postmodernism in strategic management.
2 The creation of strategies is a cognitive process, the strategic map in the minds of managers constitutes merely an idea for organizational reality, and strategy is an emanation of the ideas of decision-makers. Information is filtered and categorized. It is easiest to accept information that is confirmed by decisions taken (consciously or not), which is an example of tendentiousness.
3 Culture, value systems, stereotypes, and the criteria of rationality all play a part in creating strategy, which is why we can call strategy a cultural creation, explained and communicated socially.
4 The social nature of strategy proves that it should be created based on the assumption of limited rationality, which also results from incomplete access to information. Strategic decisions are the result of a game that takes place in the social structures in which organizations are embedded and in the organizations themselves. Of key importance for strategy, which reflects the interdependencies between social and economic entities, is understanding power and communication.
5 Interpretative strategy features ambiguity, relativism, and ideology; uses creative and heuristic processes; and is subject to a small degree to algorithmization. The game metaphor, containing an element of uncertainty, creates a space for constructing strategy based on limited rationality. The war metaphor draws attention to emotional and ideological components, while the linguistic game highlights the interpretation processes of social actors.
6 There are also irrational aspects in understanding strategy – organizational reality is not established; it is created through interaction between managers and society. Brusson proposed recognizing decision-making irrationality, that is the position that rational decisions do not have to lead to effective actions. The researcher may have doubts, but the decision-maker must usually take a quick decision, communicate it, convince others of it, and ultimately implement it. The rationality of the decision may be overshadowed by more important elements of engagement or communication. Belief in the success of an initiative often becomes more important than long-term planning. Clarke notes that plans in a symbolic dimension may cause managerial

passivity, suggesting that the situation is under control. A similar intentional approach to strategy is proposed by the concepts of the *management of meanings*, *sensemaking*, and *sensegiving*, in which the leader influences others with his or her vision of organizational reality.

7 Emotional factors are important in taking decisions, including strategic ones. Damasio investigated the somatic marker hypothesis and argued that they play a significant role in the selection of decision variants.
8 The assumption of social constructivism blurs the boundary between the descriptive and the normative approach to strategy. Managers' ideas about strategy are a model to which organizational reality is adapted.

The interpretative paradigm of strategic management defines new functions for organizational strategy. The goal of strategy is to find and implement solutions that lead to the realization of intentions. However, strategies do not only fulfil a rational function. The intentional function involves striving to influence reality and thus contains an element of social constructivism. The intentions of planners will here be a self-fulfilling prophecy – strategists and other organizational players will believe in them. The emotive function of strategy involves connecting plans with feelings. The individual is appropriately determined in the pursuit of the goal. Emotions therefore play a motivating role for strategy builders (self-motivation) and for employees, and their reading is possible thanks to the processes of the management of meanings. The leadership function of strategy is related to the existence in the organization of a stable and effective power structure, setting goals and ensuring their achievement. Employees look at organizational coherence through the lens of strategy. The communication function determines the necessity for organization members to negotiate and transfer information regarding choices (*sensemaking*, *sensegiving*). It can clearly be seen that strategy is based on not only rational decisions but also the creation of organizational reality, that is the fundamental element of organizational identity and culture.

Within the organization there are strategic processes that can be redefined from the point of view of alternative paradigms, in particular interpretivism. Let us enumerate six such examples:

Allocation of Strategic Resources

Decision-makers personally determine the organization's strategic resources (including financial, knowledge, material, and human) and the rules for their allocation. Every resource can be managed in a different way depending on the adopted interpretation. Here, one can use the triad: exploitation-protection-development. Through exploitation, a resource is used up but nevertheless has an impact on the organization's development. Protection involves conserving a resource, while development involves striving to increase the size of the resource. The way a resource is managed is impacted by the processes of interpretation as well as negotiation and projection.

The organization's vision and mission usually constitute the projection of decision-makers' ideas, which builds organizational identity and sets the direction for employees' efforts. It is managers, as part of creative processes, who select areas for activity and the most important goals. The creation of a mission involves indicating the direction for development and its boundary conditions. It is characterized by intentionality and therefore influences thinking with regard to the organization. On the one hand it directs thinking towards specific activity, while on the other it may not allow for advantage to be taken of opportunities outside the leading area. Contemporary management concepts draw attention to symbolic resources: intellectual and social capital. Changing the organization's mission may be problematic as it is treated like an organizational constitution, and any change is seen as a sign of revolution. A change of mission usually involves a change of managers.

The mission is imagined by the organization's members to be the source of its market power and constitutes an analogy to Ricardo's 'comparative advantage', thus resulting from perception and interpretation. This analogy suggests that the market position has not been achieved by chance. Employees are convinced that the organization's success is the result of a unique combination of strategic resources. Competitive advantage is the interplay of numerous competitive elements, for example, the idea and the loyalty of both clients and employees.

These concepts show that strategic management is entangled in culture, as 'competitive advantage' is not free of ethnocentrism. The American approach, which is competitive and individualistic, may be hard to fit in to cooperative and collectivist categories. An advantage over others is not always essential; sometimes it is enough to find one's own domain or market niche.

Strategic management theory makes use of numerous models and ideas. While the concepts of Drucker, Porter, Ansoff, Kotler, and others assigned to strategy schools are used in practice, this usually brings uncertainty as to the selection of a cognitively effective concept. Decision-makers may make use of several solutions: from deciding on one model, through hybrids of several models, even to ignoring theory and using common sense and intuition. The choice of concept and its reading are areas of the interpretative trend.

A decision regarding the strategic concept reducing uncertainty leads to the definition of strategic options (e.g. in the sectoral model). Managers' thinking is structured according to the content of the adopted theory. The sectoral model can help us visualize the available strategic options, among which managers must make a choice (e.g. cost economy). If the strategic options take the form of a dichotomy (e.g. cost economy), this will have an impact on simplifying decision-makers' perception of organizational reality – according to the interpretative assumption that language influences our choices and constitutes the cognitive boundaries of our world. This does not mean that the framework of theories and options to choose from is insurmountable. For example, decision-makers may see the possibility to concurrently implement several strategic options or may propose their own solutions. Despite this, the chosen concept will determine their way of thinking and the path of interpretation. Strategy is created through action, thus in implementing intentions it may turn out to be necessary to modify them considerably. Development of the organization (verified through comparison to the competition) constitutes here the basic determinant to which strategy adjustments are subordinated.

The concept of the interpretative understanding of an organization's strategy illustrated here is, in my opinion, closer to organizational life than hyperrational models. Indicating the stages to strategic processes is a difficult task. Crucial here are organizational actions related to the interdependent elements of perception, interpretation, communication, and the rationalization of action. Both cognitive research dedicated to planning processes and the mind and management practice rather prove retrospective interpretation than perspective strategy planning. Actions are not the result of the planning process; they are related to the processes of organizational reality.

Strategic planning constitutes a process of predicting and creating the future, as well as matching organizational actions to it. Strategic management theory places emphasis on the rational aspects of planning, that is on knowledge. The more data there is about the organization and the surroundings, the more effective planning will be. Knowledge increases the probability of strategic planning. Despite this it is not devoid of social and emotional elements, for example, belief in the success of the chosen variant. Managerial activity draws on knowledge from the field of management and related disciplines and also the belief in the sense of the actions taken and in the legitimacy of one's own interpretation of organizational reality. This belief combines the individual dimension (individual beliefs) and the collective dimension (socio-cultural). Belief in strategic management means a set of conscious and unconscious norms, values, and cultural patterns that make up managerial identity. A manager must be convinced that they will achieve the vision they set for themselves. This gives them determination and increases their engagement which they can then use to 'infect' their employees (*sensemaking, sensegiving*). Strategy achievement therefore contains components of knowledge and belief. This dialectic was long disregarded in strategic management, in which the dominant trends glorified only the rational factors of strategic planning, without attaching importance to socio-emotional aspects. Exceptions include the concepts of logical incrementalism, emergent strategies, and symbolic action strategies. For four decades, strategic management has also seen an emphasis on the role of intuition, emotions, and 'hidden knowledge'.

13 Paradigm Shifts in Organizational Culture

The concept of organizational culture comes on the one hand from the multiple meanings of the cultural trend, while on the other it is the derivative of understanding organizational reality in anthropological and sociological categories. The multiplicity of interpretations of the meaning of organizational culture encourages the adoption of an open position. The importance of culture also depends on the interpreter as well as on the context in which it is used. Theorists define culture according to the adopted paradigm, while practitioners more often reach for its instrumental understanding. This results in the need for discussion on the adopted definition of organizational culture before the commencement of research or analyses.

The concept of culture creates a wide-ranging 'family of terms' that complicates operationalization; however, these are used very often in management – as a metaphor, theory, or in empirical research. A certain 'fashion' for organizational culture has existed in management for more than three decades, and if we look to the beginning of the cultural trend in management, it has a tradition going back over 70 years. Although knowledge management concepts redirect the focus from values and norms to cognition, researchers and managers often refer to culture in interpreting an enterprise's success or failure (Al Saifi 2015). The theory of organizational culture gives rise to many epistemological dilemmas. Under the cover of popularity there are problems in understanding and managing culture. It is worth analysing the cognitive problems of organizational culture in management and making an attempt to resolve them.

Let us list the five most characteristic issues. These are:

1 The varied, ambiguous, and unclear definitions of organizational culture;
2 The contradictions (or incommensurability) of organizational culture paradigms;
3 The lack of agreement among researchers as to the model and typology of organizational culture (its dimensions, variables, components, and levels);
4 The differently understood dependencies between organizational culture and structure, strategy, and the organization's surroundings;

DOI: 10.4324/9781003530947-17

5 The development and popularity of similar concepts (organizational identity and atmosphere).

The ways of defining organizational culture, as well as its paradigms, cause the cultural trend many problems. This is also related to the ambiguity of cultural research as such. We can point to numerous paradigms for understanding both culture and organizational culture. In terms of culture, it is worth noting the following trends: functionalist-structuralist (NFS), interpretative-symbolic (IS), postmodernism (also defined as radical humanism), and poststructuralism (related to the critical trend – CMS).

In classical management trends from the first half of the 20th century, the organizational culture trend did not exist. The IS paradigm, referring to the symbolic interactionism initiated by GH Mead, understood organizational culture as the process of creating and reading organizational reality, manifesting itself in linguistic and symbolic actions of individuals in the group, which can be investigated using qualitative methods. The possibility of the instrumental shaping of organizational culture was approached with scepticism. Modernism viewed organizational culture through the lens of structuralist and functionalist categories as a subsystem of the organization that could be subject to comparative research and saw the need to control it and in effect instrumentalize it. Postmodernism drew attention to defragmentation, textualism, the narrative approach, and cultural and epistemological relativism and negated the meaning of methodology – the proper 'anti-method' was deconstruction.

Smircich provides an insight into paradigms that are the basis for concepts linking culture and organization (Smircich 1983, pp. 160–172) and indicates five common areas:

1 The cognitive theory of the organization;
2 Comparative cross-cultural research;
3 Organizational symbolism;
4 The internal culture of the enterprise;
5 Subconscious and unconscious processes in the organization (Table 13.1).

Organizational culture can be understood as an independent variable (external, due to the influence of the surroundings), an internal variable of the organization, and also a core metaphor. In comparative cross-cultural research in management it is an independent variable that influences the organization. It is perceived in functionalist categories. In this context, research has been conducted into social and national management styles as well as comparative research on the impact of the context of culture on the organization. Culture as an internal variable is the result of the actions taken by the organization, for which it is specific and by which it is shaped. Research focuses on creating and developing culture, its typologies, and its connections with organizational effectiveness. In

Table 13.1 Typology of cultural research in management

Culture as an independent variable	*Culture as an internal variable*	*Culture as a core metaphor*
Cross-cultural management National management styles Similarities and differences in management in different countries The relationship between effectiveness and national culture The globalization of organizational culture	**Company culture** Managing company culture The relationship between effectiveness and organizational culture Changes to and classification of organizational cultures	**Cognitive approach** The organization as a cognitive undertaking **Symbolistic approach** The organization as a symbolic discourse **Dramaturgical approach** People as organizational actors The organization as theatre **Interpretative approach** Organizational reality as an intentional construct of consciousness **Psychodynamic approach** Investigating the organization as a form of human expression
FUNCTIONALISM		**NON-FUNCTIONALIST PARADIGMS**

Source: Own elaboration.

categories of non-functionalist paradigms, culture is a core metaphor, identical to the organization, which constitutes a set of symbolic actions, a form of human expression, a cognitive undertaking, and the manifestation of the deep structures of the mind. In the paradigms described, a change of perspective occurs. Organizations are no longer simply an economic undertaking, and attention is drawn to the psychological, social, and symbolic aspects of their functioning.

Martin makes a classification of organizational culture concepts on the basis of the opinions of over 70 researchers, including them in one of three theoretical perspectives (Martin 2002, pp. 93–114):

- The integration perspective – which strives for the stability and uniformity of organizational culture (similarities to the functionalist structuralist paradigm);
- The differentiation perspective – possible are divisions, conflicts, subcultures, and separations (close to the IS paradigm);
- The fragmentation perspective – directed toward division and change in culture (close to postmodernism and poststructuralism).

Other researchers also present their own proposals for approaches to organizational culture; however, they often forget that the foundations of organizational culture should be sought in culture as such.

This diffusion of both organizational culture paradigms and meanings generates difficulties in creating coherent research programmes. The concept of culture is extremely broad. For example, in the cultural trend there is no accumulation of scientific achievements, and researchers representing different schools and paradigms do not make use of each other's research. The relationships of culture with other elements of the organization (its surroundings, structure, or strategy) also remain undefined. This issue is approached in different ways depending on the research perspective.

The first issue is the differentiation of organizational culture from other areas of the organization. Functionalists opt for dividing the cultural sphere from the structural and strategic sphere, while interpretivists and postmodernists allow for, and sometimes postulate, the interweaving of these areas.

The next problem is determining the superiority of organizational culture in relation to other management spheres. We refer here to Drucker's well-known statement that 'culture eats strategy for dinner'. The majority of culture researchers proclaim the superiority or at least the equivalent of culture in management. However, outside the cultural trend there is no lack of supporters of the predominance of strategy over organizational culture.

The third issue is the relationship between organizational culture and the organization's socio-economic surroundings. The subject literature abounds with research and analyses into the dependencies between the surroundings and culture in general, such as the classic studies by Weber (2002), the analyses of the relationship between culture and the wealth of nations by Fukuyama (2001) and Landes (2000), and the comparative cross-cultural research by House, Inglehart, Hofsted, Trompenaars, and Hampden-Turner. The majority of researchers recognize the diffusion of values from the culture of societies to organizational culture (Haldin-Herrgard 2000). The inverse effect can also take place, however, to a lesser degree due to the size of the collective and powerfully rooted norms. However, we have still not seen a dominating model that presents these dependencies, such as the possibility for assessing the degree of coherence between both cultures. Some authors describe culture using different models and value dimensions, and others recognize greater coherence and use the same or similar models. The lack of guidelines separating organizational culture from other elements of the organizational system and the surroundings leads to the use of varied research and practical assumptions. This is why theorists and managers have a dual approach – sceptical or enthusiastic – to managing organizations using organizational culture.

Another problem is differentiating models of organizational culture from models of culture as such. It is hard to isolate organizational culture from the organizational system as a whole, which is why it is not easy to classify and describe it. Mintzberg speaks of five organizational configurations (the divided form, professional bureaucracy, simple structure, the bureaucratic machine, and adhocracy), and although he focuses on the structure, he also refers to a large degree to organizational culture. Perrow created a technology matrix based on the parameters of the variability and analysability of tasks (routine, non-routine, engineering, crafted), indicating at the same time the types of organizational culture. The sita and human capital model is also an organizational culture model with its opposing types of ideals. It is no different with models of power, human resource management, leadership, and organizational learning – they constitute a description of the whole organization or its selected aspect and model (or typology) of organizational culture. The ambiguity of organizational culture concepts makes it practically impossible to separate organizational culture from other spheres of the organization.

In terms of the division of organizational culture, most popular are the theories of Deal and Kennedy, Schein, Ouchi, Hofsted, Peters and Waterman, and Handy, based on functional structuralism and in accordance with the issue of the components of organizational culture. Many authors, following Schein, enumerate several elements of organizational culture from among rituals, norms, values, assumptions, language, cultural patterns, symbols, artefacts, and taboos (Schein 1992). Deal and Kennedy differentiate organizational cultures in terms of the degree of risk and the pace of verification of managerial decisions. As a result of the intersection of these dimensions, we obtain a typology of cultures: strong guys (macho), pouring all their energy into their firm, working hard and playing hard, and process-oriented (Deal, Kennedy 1988). The ideas of Handy, Ouchi, and Peters and Waterman can be considered as similar simplifications, without a background in the form of broader research projects. The above-mentioned concepts are more like examples of 'marketing products', that is guidebooks based on a spectacular idea and widely popularized, but often unfortunately overly trivial without reliable empirical foundations despite the impression of brilliance. The same cannot be said in the case of Hofsted's concept, which was constructed thanks to research into enterprises based on a qualitative-quantitative research programme. It distinguishes six dimensions of organizational culture analysis (Hofstede 1984):

- Open system – closed system;
- Procedure-oriented – result-oriented;
- Loose control – tight control;
- Professionalism – affiliation;
- Pragmatism – normativity;
- Care for employees – care for production.

However, these dimensions are completely different from the proposals of other authors who also developed their models on the basis of empirical research (Goffee, Jones 1998). We therefore have to come to terms with the diversity of models, dimensions, and typologies for organizational cultures.

Among the dimensions of organizational culture considered we often have the following dichotomies:

1 Conservative culture – innovative culture;
2 Weak culture – strong culture;
3 Collectivist culture – individualistic culture;
4 Negative culture – positive culture;
5 Hierarchical culture – egalitarian culture;
6 Introvert culture – extrovert culture;
7 Bureaucratic culture – pragmatic culture.

The challenge remains the different selection of dimensions and their different understanding. For example, the division weak culture – strong culture to some speaks of homogeneity, while to others it speaks of organizational effectiveness.

Organizational culture researchers suggest a broad range of cognitive, pragmatic, quantitative, and qualitative methods. The most notable include survey questionnaires, used in particular in international comparative projects and in qualitative analyses of the organization (to complement case studies). Speaking of research into organizational cultures, we must mention organizational anthropology methods (organizational ethnology). Smircich, Rosen, Hatch, Czarniawska, and Kostera have proven that engaged and participatory methods originating in cultural anthropology can be applied (Hatch 1997, pp. 275–288). It is especially worth taking into account such techniques as text analysis, in-depth interviews, participatory observation, and methodologies related to organizational anthropology and originating in sociology: ethnomethodology, the sociology of intervention, grounded theory, etc.

Since the application of so many research methods is recommended, can we speak of the coherence of research results? Researchers demonstrating the relationship between their research and organizational culture do in fact investigate cultural norms, structure, communication, and power in the organization. No paradigm has proposed a methodology for synthesizing organizational culture, thanks to which it would be possible to predict changes in culture. We can therefore say that cognitive methods of managing organizational culture have at their disposal a rather moderate diagnostic and prognostic power.

As a result of conducting quantitative research, we obtain a description of organizational cultures in the form of several dimensions, which does not allow for a complete understanding of the above-mentioned norm systems, power relations, or communication processes. Thanks to anthropological research into the organization we obtain descriptive, dispersed, and unrepresentative case studies, thus although the insight is deeper, we cannot talk of generalization. The value of these studies is often the discovery of camouflaged networks of meanings based on the conflicting interests or on power relations. Such research reveals a specific configuration of meanings that remains elusive in quantitative or representative research, which often constitutes a projection of the researcher's own concepts (Janićijević 2011, pp. 69–99).

The next problem is the limited number and scope of research programmes (Denison 1996, pp. 619–654). Very few complex, reliable long-term research projects and international studies of organizational culture have been conducted, despite the fact that we can boast numerous international projects researching the cultures of societies. The diffusion of researchers' efforts means the fragmentation of knowledge on organizational culture.

The lack of agreement as to the paradigm, definition model, and typology of organizational culture (also within the same paradigm) has negative effects on the research programme and practical applications. Researchers must define organizational culture for the needs of individual analyses, and thus, there is no cumulation and incommensurable research results often occur.

Pragmatic methodology is supposed to facilitate effective management of organizational culture, and thus, methods for improving the organization should lead to an increase in its effectiveness and better achievement of goals. In organizational culture, this methodology is not as well developed as cognitive research methodology but includes diagnosis of the existing cultural configuration and also planning changes to it, conducting cultural intervention, and controlling the whole process. Shaping organizational culture turns out to be difficult due to its variability, ambiguity, and unconsciousness nature. Functionalists approach the possibility of diagnosis and cultural intervention more optimistically than interpretivists, sometimes believing in 'engineering organizational culture'. Postmodernists do not assume the option of controlling changes in cultural processes at all. Among the methods and techniques of creating organizational culture are activities relating to cultural processes and activities regarding other elements of the organization, which subsequently influence culture. Diagnostic methods include primarily organizational culture audits, placing culture on the map and in a specific typology within the adopted model.

Methods of planning cultural change usually aim to identify an ideal model of organizational culture, which will be possible to implement through a transformation programme. Intervention methods strive to change values, norms, assumptions, and the remaining elements of culture according to an assumed pattern. The most popular pragmatic techniques for managing culture at the level of diagnosis include in-depth and focused interviews, surveys, and questionnaires for cultural auditing. Helpful in planning cultural change are brainstorms, Delphic rounds, and expert panels, while the techniques of cultural intervention include transformation of the human resource management system, employee training, changes in organizational rules and organizational symbols (logos, brands, etc.), introducing agents of change, mentoring and a change of leadership, and transformation of the mission as well as the communication system and the organizational structure (O'Donovan 2006). Following a wave of optimism related to the effectiveness of tools for change in organizational culture comes their limited application due to a low level of effectiveness. Shaping organizational culture has no effective power like strategic or structural aspects (managers can create strategies and structure projects unhindered as well as control their implementation to a certain degree). Changes and intervention in organizational culture usually have limited effectiveness. We do not have research at our disposal indicating whether certain methods of making cultural change in the organization exist, nor what their impact is on increasing the organization's effectiveness.

The lack of universal methods is the result of the many paradigms and the methodological eclecticism in the cultural trend. This may also constitute a feature of cultural research as such – it is difficult to indicate cases of effective intervention or prognosis of revolutionary cultural change. Cultural research focuses primarily on post factum description and diagnosis.

The problems of pragmatic methodology also include the dominance of consulting and popularizing concepts, which conduct excessive simplifications of the cultural phenomena of organizing and cannot respond to the actual needs of managers. Methods of managing organizational culture are often only intellectual products that gain passing popularity and which have no real application in practice. Marketing ideas, consulting, and business gurus often deflect attention away from valuable research projects. The Burrell and Morgan Matrix seems to respond to the needs of organizational culture as it constitutes a multi-paradigm description of cultural processes in the organization.

As it is so hard to understand and even more difficult to control, is it worth researching organizational culture at all? Analysis of the achievements of the cultural trend in management may help us to answer this question. Problems of definition do not undermine the importance of the trend.

Firstly, the cultural trend proposed reliable research into cultural differentiation in societies and organizations, which impacts the enterprise, economic development, and employee actions. Many research projects describe the differentiation of cultural patterns, norms, and organizational values, demonstrating the considerable influence of the cultural context of society (Sweeney, Hardaker 1994). This leads to the consideration of cultural relativism, which polemicizes with the remnants of neopositivist thinking that lies at the basis of the historical 'scientific management' trend.

Secondly, the cultural trend drew attention to the differentiation in management tools originating in different cultures and the possibility for their adaptation to other social conditions. Management techniques already developed by one society can be applied in others, of course with certain limitations. The use of Japanese organizational techniques (quality circle, *kaizen*, *kanban*) in American or European conditions is an example of the problematic differences in cross-cultural management.

Thirdly, the cultural trend contributed to the development of this very subdiscipline of management – cross-cultural management. The processes of globalization have caused a rise in the importance of transnational corporations. The emergence of subsidiaries, branches, strategic alliances, and mergers has had an impact on the development of cross-cultural and organizational culture communication tools, e.g. training systems, cultural audits, and techniques for the transformation of values, norms, and cultural patterns. Research into the influence of a society's culture on enterprises has turned out to be crucial in the globalization of economic activity, which has borne fruit in the form of the development of cross-cultural management.

Fourthly, the cultural approach has encouraged the search for ever newer ways of understanding the organization and economic life and for undertaking epistemological discussion. It has demonstrated the fallibility of the *homo oeconomicus* assumption, proposing instead reflection referring to two perspectives: functionalist and non-functionalist. In the epistemological and methodological spheres, management found itself in the family of social sciences and the humanities.

Fifthly, thanks to the cultural trend, the methodological scope of research into the organization has been broadened, mainly by the inclusion of interpretative methods. A place has therefore been found for 'soft' research methods (projection techniques, biographical and focused interviews, discursive and narrative methods, and ethnomethodological techniques). Qualitative methods were no longer exclusively an introduction to representative research (Walker, Symon, Davies 1996, pp. 96–105).

Therefore, as the cultural trend in management can be assessed positively, how should research be conducted in this area? It is certainly not worth questioning the multiplicity of organizational culture paradigms and definitions but adopting a position of pluralism and methodological eclecticism, being open to concepts and methods from other scientific disciplines not only from the social sciences and the humanities but also from the exact sciences (cognitive science, information technology, neuroscience, evolutionary psychology) (Hatch, Schultz 1996, pp. 529–557). Analysis of cultural processes may become part of a scientific revolution, connecting issues of the social sciences and the natural sciences with one another. It is worth continuing research in the field of organizational culture in order to have criteria for rejecting concepts of low cognitive value or without credible empirical research.

A solution to the problem of the differentiation of organizational culture could be multi-paradigm analysis. What prejudgements can we mention in the context of organizational culture? Thinking drawn from the exact, technical, and economic sciences means perceiving organizational culture in analytical and operationalist categories and thus assumes the possibility of separating it from other organizational components, managing it, and predicting the directions of its development as well as its precise definition and measurement. This is a tendency to understand organizational culture on the basis of the NFS paradigm. However, there is often scepticism as to the cognitive value of functionalist concepts of organizational culture. Representatives of the social sciences and the humanities often perceive culture through the lens of the IS paradigm, radical structuralism, or even radical humanism. In this case, organizational culture is a core metaphor of the organization as a whole, in which structure and strategy are not separated from one another, the ambiguity and inconsistency of research results is allowed, and less belief is placed in management and control of organizational culture. Theorists and managers have different intellectual backgrounds. The impact of education is filtered by professional and life experience, which perpetuates or eliminates our beliefs. In the case of organizational culture, experience forms our deep belief in issues of exercising influence on people, their behaviours, and value systems. We will therefore understand organizational culture either in a universalistic and in a scientistic manner, or we will be supporters of relativism and the ambiguity of these concepts. Understanding culture in general also becomes important as it constitutes a certain pattern for understanding organizational culture. If we perceive culture as civilization, with its technological-material aspects, this automatically brings us closer to functionalist-structuralist theories of organizational culture. An awareness of the ambiguity of understanding culture leads us to adopt non-functionalist paradigms.

Many authors attempt to explore organizational culture using metaphors, analogies, paradoxes, and symbols. G. Morgan proposed looking at culture as a metaphor for the organization in general, which was also adopted by other researchers, including Smircich, Czarniawska, and Kostera. Organizational culture has also been described as organizational glue, a text, a mental programme, theatre, or even a happening. Deal and Kennedy, as well as Handy, propose a typology for culture full of symbols. These include the symbol of the spider's web, analogies to Greek gods, and comparisons to social roles, thanks to which the most important features of a given cultural configuration can be quickly and precisely understood. A metaphorical understanding of organizational culture referring to humanistics, in particular hermeneutics, allows complex meanings to be captured. In addition, it constitutes an example of using the apparatus of art and aesthetics in interpreting social reality. Many researchers, primarily interpretivists, agreed that managing organizational culture is also an art due to the intuitiveness, the role of tacit knowledge, and the creativity of management. We immerse ourselves in culture, we interpret it, and we operate within it, either habitually or reflexively. Intuition is helpful in every case as it facilitates taking decisions, convincing others of their suitability, and implementing them. In the opinion of the majority of interpretivists and postmodernists, the sphere of cultural management cannot be controlled and has weak predictive power as it rather involves creativity and creating social reality than determined social engineering contained in action algorithms.

Shaping organizational culture possesses axiological, aesthetic, and praxeological aspects and is a valuing activity. Building organizational identity around given values is not without consequences for all stakeholders. It is necessary to remember about the development of such values and norms as social responsibility, the subjective treatment of employees, etc.

The axiology of organizational culture refers to the idea of 'goods', while the aesthetics of art also refers to the idea of 'beauty'. Aesthetics is very important for culture as in both there is the creation of beauty and its antithesis. For this reason, the derivative of culture, that is organizational culture, cannot be devoid of aesthetic ideals. Although there are a few aesthetic threads in management, they do appear in the context of organizational culture. Organizational anthropology is increasingly becoming the basis for documenting texts classified as specific organizational literature Cultural diagnosis reaches for organizational stories, role-playing, and spectacles.

The praxeology of organizational culture views it through the lens of the efficiency function. Praxeology is related to the practical nature of this issue, thanks to which organizational culture research can be distinguished from analyses of culture as such. Cultural studies do not have to adopt a praxeological orientation, but research into organizational culture does, especially when it constitutes a subject of management science.

14 Paradigm Shifts in Marketing

In the management science family, marketing is one of the most rapidly developing subdisciplines and the subject of interest of many people, despite the fact that it only crystallized as a scientific discourse after the Second World War (Shaw, Tamilia 2001, pp. 156–163). The impact of cognitive marketing activity is visible in the practical aspect. Meanwhile, in the epistemological sense, marketing enables economic entities to get to know and initiate relationships with other entities, which is intended to contribute to their economic success (Workman Jr, Homburg, Gruner 1998, pp. 21–41). Marketing is present not only in the economy but also in the political and social activity (Donovan, Henley 2003). The research fields and subject of marketing are continually undergoing change, which can be perceived as damaging for the identity of the discipline but at the same time indicates the dynamic development of the science (Alsem, Kostelijk 2008). It is characterized by pragmatic (to a large degree borrowed) and eclectic methodology, as well as interdisciplinarity, since many problems also function in other sciences: economics, the sociology of organizations, cultural anthropology, etc. Also debatable is the division of theory from practice, the definition of the role of the researcher-theorist, and marketing practice. Questions about the identity of the subdiscipline lead to continuous epistemological reflection, manifesting itself amongst others in self-criticism and a cyclical cognitive crisis (Van Heerde, Helsen, Dekimpe 2007, pp. 230–245).

Marketing is treated as a 'science' due to its fulfilling institutional and social criteria (presence in the academic discourse – journal publication, conferences, academic degrees and hierarchies, and specializations – as well as recognition by theorists and practitioners). However, some perceive marketing as a practical activity that merely makes use of scientific methods. The position of epistemological and methodological pluralism, as well as the multi-paradigm and poly-methodological nature of the social sciences, enable us to firmly believe that marketing is a science belonging to management science, that is a science according to social and historical criteria, not the neopositivist ideals of the natural sciences. Let us consider marketing as a multi-paradigm science that has much in common with sociology and economics. Meanwhile, in the methodological

DOI: 10.4324/9781003530947-18

sphere, similarly to many other management disciplines, marketing draws both on the social sciences (e.g. the survey method from sociology and the case method from law) from the humanities (organizational anthropology) as well as from the natural sciences (methods for researching the brain i.e. MRI, PET).

The neopositivist-functionalist-systemic paradigm continues to dominate in marketing due to the fact that researchers attempt to understand reality in quantitative frameworks, using cause-and-effect variables and dependencies. Practical marketing concepts draw on the economic rationality of human behaviour, and their methods aim to lead to obtaining an objective picture that enables predicting the future, the creation of marketing strategies, and the taking of managerial decisions. It turns out to be necessary to process a huge amount of market data, which is then subject to algorithmic procedures. Relationship marketing, marketing-mix, and targeting have achieved the status of scientific theory (micro- or medium range), to which the correspondence concept of truth can be applied. The task of promotion-mix and marketing communication is to provide managers with knowledge of the features of a product aimed at specific buyers. The methods applied in marketing usually contribute to reducing the complexity of the process by depriving it of a social dimension; although at the same time, the branch of social marketing is also developing (Wood 2012).

However, it may be that the dominating *homo oeconomicus* model will encounter cognitive difficulties. Buyers are not always characterized by rationality, emotions are used in the creation of brands, meanings and symbols are employed in marketing communication, while sales are subject to consumer fashion. Even the processing of a huge amount of data does not always result in effective decision-making. It is also difficult to verify the scientific status of some marketing 'theories'.

In marketing, the interpretative-symbolic paradigm approach is effective in research into:

- Marketing communication;
- Consumption;
- Relationship marketing;
- The brand effect.

A. Venkatesh speaks of the phenomenon of the 'economy of symbols', which is post-material in nature. Consumers purchase brands and along with them meanings that require cultural interpretation (Kadirov, Varey 2011, pp. 160–171). Marketing communication takes place primarily in the symbolic world. Symptoms of the functioning of marketing as symbolic communication include the increasing role of fashion and brands and the domination of services in the economy. Marketing provides symbolic meanings related to consumption that spread throughout society. In the economics of modernism, material and measurable factors are responsible for economic growth, not incidental factors such as meanings or symbols. Despite their cultural, variable, and subjective nature, brands have conquered the world and defied the rigours of modernism. The increasing importance of fashion, counterculture. and irony in building brands are symptoms of symbolic marketing. The interpretative approach to advertising is moving away from the classical model of conveying information and influencing potential clients and instead uses symbols and the possibility of reading them.

Radical structuralism is indirectly present in marketing theory and practice, in analyses of the critical trend in management science. In management, sociology, and ethics literature we also find publications of an anti-marketing nature, which show it as a science and social practice characterized by manipulation and exploitation. PR, CSR, and branding can be treated as 'fashionable' tools for manipulating people's consciousness and collective identity, which below the surface serve the interests of corporations. The foundations of marketing are also criticized, which are supposed to be an ideology that preserves power and the existing social order (Eckhardt, Dholakia, Varman 2013, pp. 7–12). In some analyses we also find proposals for ethical marketing related to responsibility and sustainable development as well as built on the subjective treatment of clients and those being researched.

The postmodernist approach appeared in marketing in the late 1980s and early 1990s along with the ideas of the network society and consumerism. Marketing authors belonging to the postmodernist trend include Brown, Venkatesh, Shultz, Fuat Firat, Clifford (Fuat Firat, Venkatesh 1993, pp. 227–249), and Holbrook (1995, pp. 128–163).

In seeking metaphors, postmodernist marketing reaches for the concepts of Baudrillard, Derrida, Lyotard, and Guattari. Postmodernists call the world of consumption culture hyperreality, which can be described using a 'simulacrum', being a kind of game, simulating actions that do not cover up any reality but are merely a manifestation of expression and self-replication. Some researchers see a simulacrum in the creation and promoting of brands. Marketing according to postmodernism therefore consists of creating an artificial and textual world of meanings and senses (Skålén, Hackley 2011, pp. 189–195). However, the growth of marketing is spontaneous in nature, and it is therefore difficult to control or to predict the direction it will follow. Creating and promoting new meanings can be done at the same time as changing or deconstructing existing ones. Marketing discourse can be informed by the metaphor of a 'rhizome' devoid of boundaries that grows, develops, and intersects everywhere (Deleuze, Guattari 2004). In marketing, we are therefore dealing with the opposition of the NFS paradigm (which dominates) and alternative paradigms. Experience leads us to expect dynamic development in marketing research using alternative concepts. The number of publications dedicated to marketing from the perspective of the critical trend is growing. Only postmodernism seems to be losing in importance in marketing, as it is in many other social science research fields.

In marketing management, we most often have a rationalistic image of an economic entity functioning on the market and striving for success by identifying and satisfying clients' needs. Nevertheless, examples of interpretative, critical, and even postmodernist thinking are also entering marketing theory and practice. In my view, the strength of marketing is its epistemological and methodological pluralism; although due to its interdisciplinarity we may face a blurring of the identity of the subdiscipline.

Part IV

Paradigms of the Future in Management Science

15 Digital Transformation in Management

Digital transformation means that new science in management has produced a profound and radical change in how an organization acts, makes decisions, and creates value for consumers. It hence includes embedding digital technologies into all business dimensions, which naturally provokes profound changes in strategies, organizational structures, processes, and cultural patterns. More than just technological change, digital transformation implies business adoption of an all-encompassing new strategy in thought and operations for fully unlocking opportunities opened by digital breakthroughs. So, the impact of digital transformation on management is crucial both in theory and in practice. We could emphasize that digital transformation is the source of new paradigm in management science building orientation towards research and practice of management in areas and with methodologies using artificial intelligence (AI), machine learning (ML), internet of things (IoT), big data analytics, and cloud computing.

In practice, in this modern and highly competitive business environment, companies are demanded to expose themselves to digital transformation to stay in line with their competitors. Some technology advancements – AI, ML, big data analytics, and cloud computing – have played significant roles in changing the corporate world by creating new opportunities and challenges. Companies not embracing digital transformation become obsolete and ancient as the more agile and creative competitors gain a larger market share (Westerman et al. 2014). More so, this solves the increasing pressure from customers for simple, personalized, efficient services. E-commerce social media and mobile technology have empowered the customer more, leading to accelerated choices and heightened expectations. Organizations would have to adapt to these changes by applying digital strategies that would help them increase their customer experience and loyalty (Vial 2019).

These are the crucial drivers for digital transformation in organizations.

- Technological Advancements: Since big data, AI, ML, and cloud computing are advancing continuously, this equips an organization with tools that will

DOI: 10.4324/9781003530947-20

raise the level of productivity, decide smarter, and serve a customer base in a better way.
- Customer Expectation: Changes in how a customer expects to be served have come about with the advent of the digital era. Consequently, businesses have to provide services personalized to individual demands that are continuously available and instantly responsive.
- Competition: Businesses are under the threat of intense competition from technology-savvy companies, as well as veteran companies adopting digital approaches, pushing them towards innovation and constantly keeping a competitive advantage.
- Operational Efficiency: Organizations can be enabled to streamline their operations, reduce costs, and increase outputs through automation and data-driven insights. Operational efficiency is the organization's capability to optimize their operations, save expenses, and enhance production through utilizing automation and data-driven insights (Fitzgerald et al. 2014).

A good number of challenges facing digitization can be brought to light in the literature. There are many benefits of digital transformation, but it likewise brings about a set of significant challenges. Cultural resistance may be developed in a workplace from fear of job loss, inadequate knowledge of digital technologies, or affection for habituated processes. To assist employees to remove this very resistance, successful techniques for change management and methods of continuous learning are needed by managers (Kane et al. 2015b). Organizations are exposed to cybersecurity risks due to an increased reliance on digital technologies. They have put in place stringent measures to protect sensitive information and maintain the confidence of their customers (Von Solms, Van Niekerk 2013). Implementing new digital technology into existing legacy systems is complex and costly. Organizations need to carefully develop and implement integration strategies so that they do not cause downtime (Davenport, Westerman 2018). Digital transformation influences the design of organizations. The process of change through digital transformation comprises changing the traditional design of an organizational structure to be more fluid, flexible, and networked. A more significant shift can thus be achieved toward fast decision-making, increased collaboration, and flexibility of response to market changes (Besson, Rowe 2012). Digital organization change often includes matrix-line structures with cross-functional teams to break down barriers within organizations to spark creativity. These teams work on projects extending across various departments and use a broad diversity of talents and perspectives to drive digital work forward. Effective leadership is critical to successful digital transformation. Even the term "digital leadership" could be proposed. Leaders need to have an exhaustive understanding of digital technologies and positively endorse their adoption. They also should drive and guide their employees in the process of change. Digital leaders, therefore, should build a culture encouraging innovation, adaptability, and lifelong learning. Leading digital change demands that there is a need for a leader to provide an explicit vision, direct digital work toward the business purpose, and offer people what is required for them to deliver success. Leaders must equally be adaptive, open, and soundly experienced in making judgements based on evidence (Brynjolfsson, McAfee 2014; Kane et al. 2015a).

The trajectory of digital transformation will continue to be determined by emerging technology and existing trends.

1 Artificial Intelligence (AI) and Machine Learning (ML): These technologies are still perceived as the front runners that are likely to become key differentiators for corporate functions, enhancing business decision-making, and reshaping personalized customer experiences (Agrawal, Gans, Goldfarb 2018).
2 Internet of Things (IoT): This refers to the ability of companies to access, collect, and analyse data from connected devices, providing better insights to improve productivity and encourage innovation (Chui, Löffler, Roberts 2010).
3 Big Data: In management practice and science, big data is founded on the extensive analysis of large, complex datasets to drive informed decision-making, optimize operations, and uncover strategic insights.
4 Blockchain Technology: Blockchain offers strong, transparent, and tamper-proof digital transactions that will transform sectors like finance, supply chain, and healthcare (Iansiti, Lakhani 2017).
5 Augmented Reality (AR) and Virtual Reality (VR): These technologies will promote superior customer experiences, better training programs, and improved work environments (Schwab 2017).

Digital transformation signifies a significant shift in how organizations operate and compete in the digital era. This change substantially improves organizational performance, innovation, and customer satisfaction by leveraging digital technologies and implementing new organizational structures and leadership techniques. However, successful digital transformation encounters many barriers, such as cultural resistance, cybersecurity vulnerabilities, and complicated integration. Firms need to keep themselves updated in ever-changing business settings to remain competitive, adapting to rapidly changing trends and technology.

16 The Role of Big Data in Management

In today's business environment, Big Data is a game-changer that dramatically alters organizational operations, decision-making approaches, and competitive strategies. Big Data analytics is a critical component of digital transformation, introducing new ways of managing data that enable data-driven decision-making. This leads to improvements in operational efficiency, innovation, and customer satisfaction.

Big Data refers to the huge volumes of structured and unstructured data companies generated from multiple sources, including social media, transactional records, sensors, and mobile devices. Key characteristics that define Big Data are its large volume, high velocity, diverse variety, and inherent truthfulness (Laney 2001). Effectively handling and analysing such data necessitates using cutting-edge technologies and methodologies like machine learning, artificial intelligence, and advanced data analytics tools (Chen, Chiang, Storey 2012).

Big Data analytics changes the game in decision-making by providing actionable insights from deep data analysis. Dependence on data-driven approaches empowers managers to make fully informed decisions based on empirical evidence rather than intuition or experience. Predictive analytics allows organizations to forecast trends, identify threats, and act on plans to attain more favourable outcomes (Davenport 2014). Big Data also enables real-time decision-making, allowing firms to respond to market dynamics and client demands promptly. Utilizing data from many sources helps firms understand the totality of the business environment for more accurate and timely decision-making (McAfee, Brynjolfsson 2012).

Incorporating Big Data analytics into organizational processes results in better operational efficiency through resource optimization, streamlining workflows, and cost savings. For supply chain management, Big Data can be used for inventory monitoring, demand forecasting, and enhanced logistics, leading to significant cost reductions and improved service levels (Hofmann 2017). In the manufacturing sector, predictive maintenance using Big Data analytics can detect equipment failures early, reducing downtime and associated maintenance costs. Data analytics also enhances talent acquisition, employee engagement,

DOI: 10.4324/9781003530947-21

and performance management processes in human resources management (Bersin 2017).

Big Data analytics is essential for enhancing customer experiences through customized marketing, improving customer service, and fostering customer loyalty. Analyzing customer data helps businesses derive essential insights into customer preferences, behaviours, and feedback, allowing them to tailor products, services, and interactions to meet individual needs. For instance, e-commerce companies use Big Data to analyse customers' browsing and purchase histories, suggesting items more likely to be bought, thus increasing sales and customer satisfaction. In the financial services industry, Big Data plays a crucial role in detecting fraud and providing personalized financial advice to individual customers (Chen, Chiang, Storey 2012).

However, there are several issues and problems raised by mass information in management:

- Data Quality: The quality of data is crucial for successful analytics as it guarantees that data are accurate, consistent, and dependable. Incorrect data might result in wrong conclusions and poor decisions (Redman 2018).
- Data Privacy and Security: These protect against the breach of confidential information and illegal entry, which is a primary concern due to the increased data collection and storage (Tankard 2012).
- Skill Gaps: Many organizations need to have highly skilled professionals capable of conducting correct analysis and interpretation of Big Data. A gap in skills may act as an impediment to the proper implementation of Big Data initiatives (Manyika et al. 2011).

The direction Big Data is taking today in terms of management is dictated by enhancing technology and evolving business requirements. Methods such as machine learning and artificial intelligence continue to increase in application, enabling much more complex analyses and insightful, in-depth results (Davenport, Ronanki 2018). Efforts aimed at making data available for employees without particular expertise in organizations will enable many more employees to use data to guide their decisions can be described as "data democratisation" (Redman 2020). The growing demand for real-time data analysis will help firms make timely and informed decisions in increasingly dynamic business environments (Benoit 2019). Big Data is a powerful change driver for management, providing the potential of decisions based on data for organizations to achieve efficiency, innovation, and enhanced customer happiness. It may pose challenges regarding data quality, security, and skills gaps, but the possible advantages certainly outweigh these difficulties. To be successful in the digital marketplace, companies will need to reskill their data strategy and harness the full potential of Big Data as technological revolutions evolve.

17 The Role of Artificial Intelligence and Machine Learning in Decision-Making

Artificial intelligence (AI) and machine learning (ML) are currently leading in the digitization of management and are changing the premise through which business entities make decisions. These technologies allow firms to examine vast amounts of data, identify patterns, and make projections to help form strategic and operational decisions. AI and ML in decision-making processes represent a significant paradigm shift toward increased effectiveness, efficiency, and creativity in management paradigms. AI and ML technologies boost the process of decision-making through advanced data analytics capacities. These technologies effectively and accurately handle big data, performing far beyond human capacity for speed and accuracy (Brynjolfsson, McAfee 2017). As a result, they uncover hidden insights that would otherwise remain invisible. AI can utilize customer information to predict buying patterns, enabling companies to customize marketing campaigns. AI and ML facilitate quick decision-making due to persistent data analysis and updated insights, which is particularly relevant in volatile corporate environments where decisions must be fast (Agrawal, Gans, Goldfarb 2018). For instance, using AI analytics in financial services can detect fraudulent activities, ensuring timely response and intervention. These technologies significantly increase operational efficiency by automating repetitive operations and simplifying complex procedures. AI in the supply chain improves inventory optimization, demand forecasting, and logistics streamlining, leading to cost reduction and expanded service levels (Huang, Rust 2018). Predictive maintenance AI can predict equipment failures in the manufacturing industry, resulting in minimal downtimes and lowered maintenance costs (Lee, Kao, Yang 2014). Additionally, AI and ML increase efficiency in people management by automating staff recruitment procedures, estimating staff turnover, and identifying staff skills gaps. This enhancement leads to improved decision-making and productivity through better quality by minimizing human-related errors and biases (Davenport, Ronanki 2018).

AI is rapidly transforming the landscape of management by automating tasks, enhancing decision-making, and enabling new ways of working. AI is automating repetitive and mundane tasks, allowing managers to focus on more strategic

DOI: 10.4324/9781003530947-22

and value-added activities. This includes automating data entry, scheduling, and basic customer service interactions, leading to increased efficiency and productivity (Brynjolfsson, McAfee 2014). AI systems can analyse vast amounts of data quickly and accurately, providing managers with insights and recommendations that improve decision-making. Predictive analytics, for example, can help managers anticipate market trends, optimize supply chains, and enhance customer experiences (Davenport, Harris 2007). AI is enabling new ways of working by facilitating remote work, enhancing collaboration through digital tools, and supporting innovation. AI-powered platforms can analyse team dynamics, suggest improvements, and help managers lead more effectively (Wilson, Daugherty 2018).

Critical role of AI for digital revolution in management means not only benefits but also many challenges. The use of AI in management raises ethical and privacy issues, particularly regarding data collection and usage. Managers must ensure that AI systems are used responsibly, transparently, and in compliance with privacy regulations (Floridi et al. 2018). The adoption of AI requires managers and employees to develop new skills. There is a growing need for training and development programs to equip the workforce with the necessary technical and analytical skills (Manyika et al. 2017). Integrating AI into management practices can be expensive, requiring significant investment in technology, infrastructure, and training. Organizations must carefully consider the cost-benefit ratio and plan for a phased implementation (Westerman, Bonnet, McAfee 2014).

With AI development we can observe new trends that impact management today and in future.

- AI-Driven Personalization: AI will increasingly enable personalized experiences for customers and employees. Personalized learning and development programs, tailored customer service, and customized product recommendations will become more prevalent (Baker, Smith 2019).
- AI-Augmented Decision-Making: AI will continue to augment human decision-making by providing deeper insights and predictive capabilities. Managers will rely on AI to make more informed and strategic decisions, enhancing overall organizational performance (Rai 2020).
- Collaborative AI Systems: The future will see a rise in collaborative AI systems that work alongside humans, supporting and enhancing their capabilities. These systems will help managers lead more effectively by providing real-time feedback, coaching, and support (Wilson, Daugherty 2018).
- Ethical AI Practices: As AI becomes more integrated into management, there will be a greater focus on ethical AI practices. Organizations will need to establish clear ethical guidelines and ensure that AI systems are designed and used in ways that promote fairness, transparency, and accountability (Floridi et al. 2018).

Strategies for effective AI implementation are connecting flexible planning, with ethics and culture of innovation, balancing "hard" and "soft" factors. Organizations should develop a comprehensive AI strategy that aligns with their business goals. This involves identifying key areas where AI can add value, setting clear objectives, and creating a roadmap for implementation (Davenport, Harris 2007). To leverage AI effectively, organizations must invest in training and development programs that equip managers and employees with the necessary skills. This includes technical skills, such as data analysis and programming, and soft skills, such as critical thinking and problem-solving (Manyika et al. 2017). Managers must prioritize ethical considerations in their AI strategies. This involves establishing ethical guidelines, conducting regular audits, and ensuring that AI systems are transparent and accountable (Floridi et al. 2018). To fully realize the benefits of AI, leaders need to foster a culture of innovation. This includes encouraging experimentation, supporting cross-functional collaboration, and promoting a mindset of continuous improvement (Westerman, Bonnet, McAfee 2014).

AI and ML elevate strategic decision-making by providing actionable insights that shape the development of long-term plans and strategies. For instance, AI can analyse market trends, competitive dynamics, and customer behaviour to identify strategic opportunities and threats. Firms can improve their strategies using more efficient, data-driven approaches (Barton, Court, Elzinga 2012). Furthermore, AI-led simulations and scenario analyses enable organizations to predict the probable impacts of various strategic decisions, enhancing risk management and promoting contingency planning (Makridakis 2017). This capability is crucial in unpredictable and rapidly changing environments.

The use of AI and ML in decision-making introduces critical ethical considerations. Ensuring data privacy, mitigating algorithmic bias, and maintaining transparency are essential for the ethical and fair application of AI-driven decisions. Organizations must establish robust governance frameworks to address these concerns and ensure responsible AI system development and use (Floridi et al. 2018). For example, protecting data privacy involves safeguarding sensitive information from unauthorized access and breaches. Consistently monitoring and adjusting AI models is necessary to prevent discriminatory outcomes. Transparency in AI decision-making means making the reasoning and data used in AI judgements comprehensible to individuals or groups with a vested interest in the outcome (Binns 2018).

Despite the transformative potential of AI and ML, several obstacles and constraints need to be addressed:

- Data Quality: The effectiveness of AI models depends on the quality and availability of data. Poor-quality data can lead to inaccurate predictions and decisions (Redman 2018).

- Integration Complexity: Integrating AI and ML with existing IT systems can be complex and resource-intensive and require significant investments in technology and training (Davenport, Kirby 2016).
- Skill Gaps: There is a need for more experts with the requisite skills to design, implement, and oversee AI and ML technologies. Addressing this skills gap is crucial for the successful adoption of AI (Manyika et al. 2017).

Several new trends are expected to influence the future of AI and ML in decision-making:

- Explainable AI (XAI): There will be an increased focus on developing more transparent and interpretable AI models to foster trust and accountability (Rai 2020).
- AI Augmentation: AI technology will progressively enhance human decision-making instead of replacing it by providing tools that amplify human skills (Wilson, Daugherty 2018).
- Edge AI: This refers to implementing AI at the periphery of networks, close to the source of data generation. This approach facilitates quicker and more effective decision-making processes (Shi et al. 2016).

AI and ML are causing a significant transformation in management by altering how decisions are made. These technologies empower firms to make well-informed, streamlined, and precise decisions, improving operational efficiency, strategic planning, and customer satisfaction. However, effectively incorporating AI and ML into decision-making processes requires overcoming obstacles such as data quality issues, ethical concerns, and skills deficiencies. As AI and ML technologies continue to advance, their impact on the future of management will grow.

18 Effects of Digital Transformation on Management Science

The digital transformation process brings with it the reorganization of organizational structures, including traditional structures, to be more flexible, decentralized, and agile. Replaced by networked, collaborative organizational structures that make quick decision-making and creativity easier, this subchapter explores the profound impact of digital transformation on the structure of organizations where changes promote flexibility and durability amid constant change in business environments.

Making a Shift from the Hierarchical to Agile Structures

Traditional hierarchical structures with rigid lines of control and siloed departments are no longer appropriate to serve the vast and complex requisites of the digital age. Therefore, digital disruption requires a new agile structure focusing on speed, agility, and cross-functional teamwork (Besson, Rowe 2012). These include such agile structures as networked teams and matrix structures, which make it easier to respond to market demands or change customer preferences promptly by reducing administrative constraints and enhancing information flows.

Agile businesses are rooted in small, self-governing teams who autonomously make decisions and work independently. This calls for creativity and responsibility on the part of the team as they directly bear the consequences (Brown 2019). Besides, they fast-track responding to new opportunities or threats, thus ensuring competitive advantages to organizations in the turbulent market.

Streamlining Interdepartmental Cooperation

Digital transformation fosters cross-functional cooperation by breaking organizational barriers and creating a collaborative work environment. Collaborative technologies enable easy and efficient communication between personnel from various departments and locations (Goh, Richards 1997). This interconnection

DOI: 10.4324/9781003530947-23

fosters the exchange of diverse viewpoints and specialized knowledge, enhancing problem-solving capabilities and generating innovative solutions.

Product development processes benefit greatly from cross-functional collaboration. In a team comprising members from R&D, marketing, and customer support departments, they can collaboratively design products that better meet market expectations. This comprehensive approach ensures all aspects of the product lifecycle are considered, improving quality and reducing time to market (Tushman, Nadler 1978).

Decentralization and Empowerment

Decentralized decision-making is a principal hallmark of digital transformation. It involves the dispersion and distribution of authority and responsibility across various organizational levels, allowing staff to make decisions without seeking approval from senior executives (Mintzberg 1980). This approach expedites decision-making and enhances employee engagement and creativity, as individuals become more autonomous and motivated to act on their initiative (Gulati, Puranam, Tushman 2012).

Empowerment is especially crucial in the digital environment, where front-line employees have the closest contact with consumers and the market. Giving decision-making authority to these employees ensures that decisions are informed by relevant data, resulting in more responsive and effective actions. This, in turn, enables the optimal use of firm resources (Spreitzer 1995).

Digital Leadership and Organizational Culture

Strong digital leadership, combined with a supportive organizational culture, is essential for successful digital transformation. Digital leaders should guide themselves through the challenges of digital transformation by combining technical skills with strategic vision and the capability to handle change effectively (Westerman, Bonnet, McAfee 2014). They must create an environment that embraces innovation, welcomes ongoing learning, and takes informed risks while ensuring alignment with the firm's digital aspirations.

A digital culture promotes agility, transparency, and collaboration. Leaders exemplify these behaviours and foster a culture that encourages experimentation and treats failures as learning opportunities. Such a culture incentivizes and supports digital projects, attracting and retaining highly skilled individuals who thrive in innovative and dynamic environments (Kane et al. 2015b).

Effects on Management and Growing of Skilled People

Talent management and development strategies in the transformation process need to evolve. Organizations must instill new competencies and skills into their employees to operate successfully within the digital landscape. These skills include technological proficiencies (data analytics, AI, cybersecurity) and interpersonal abilities (flexibility, teamwork, problem-solving) (Gartner 2020).

Ongoing education and training programs are essential in helping staff acquire the necessary skills and knowledge. Organizations must build a learning culture by continuously enhancing professional growth and keeping staff updated on technical advancements. Competitive advantage is maintained through recruiting digital natives and those attuned to the vision of digital transformation, as they are naturally adept at navigating the digital age (Bersin 2017).

Though there are multiple advantages of digital transformation, the reorganization of practices by firms encounters various hurdles connected to deepness and complexities of changes. Both employees and management might resist changes due to fears of new situations, loss of power, or disruption of established patterns. Effective communication, training, and change management strategies are crucial to minimizing this resistance (Kotter 1996). Integrating new digital systems with legacy systems presents technical and financial challenges. Well-planned and strategized processes of digital transformation are necessary to prevent disruption and ensure alignment (Ross, Beath, Sebastian 2017). Implementing digital transformation projects often demands substantial financial and human resources (Fitzgerald et al. 2014). Organizations must prioritize their investments and strategically distribute resources to achieve desirable outcomes and to balance "hard" (finance, production, logistic factors) with "soft" one (people, culture, leadership).

In the digital age, organizational structures are expected to evolve into more flexible and adaptable forms. Some emerging trends include:

1 Holacracy: Some businesses are experimenting with holacracy, a system of self-management that serves as an alternative to traditional hierarchies (Robertson 2015). This approach distributes authority and decision-making across various divisions instead of centralizing control.
2 Digital Twins: Creating virtual copies of physical assets or processes can enhance organizational structures by providing real-time insights and predictive analytics (Tao et al. 2019).
3 Gig Economy and Remote Work: The rise of the gig economy and remote work is transforming organizational structures, allowing for greater flexibility and decentralization of work arrangements (Spreitzer, Cameron, Garrett 2017).

The process of digital transformation is fundamentally altering organizational structures, leading to more flexible, decentralized, and collaborative setups. These modifications enhance an organization's ability to adapt quickly, generate new ideas, and remain competitive in the digital era. However, effectively managing this shift requires addressing challenges such as resistance to change, integration complexities, and resource constraints. For sustained success, companies must adopt new structural models and cultivate an environment where digital leadership and continuous learning thrive.

Digital transformation profoundly affects the organization's employees, necessitating the redefinition of job functions and the development of new competencies. This subchapter examines what digital transformation means for employees in an organization, changes in roles, skilling/reskilling requirements, and what human resources can do in fostering these transitions. It has reshaped organizational change from traditional job roles and responsibilities. Routine and repetitive tasks are increasingly becoming automated, creating a need to shift focus towards more strategic and value-adding activities. This demands new skills for employees, who need to adapt their working methods to emphasize creativity, problem-solving, and critical thinking (Bessen 2019). This shift has led to the emergence of new job roles due to new tools and digital platforms, such as data scientists, cybersecurity analysts, and digital marketing specialists, all of which are crucial to contemporary organizational success. These roles require a blend of technical know-how and business intelligence, placing their holders in a position of lifelong learning and development to adapt to the changing world of work (Manyika et al. 2017). Organizations need to invest in upskilling and reskilling their workforce to keep pace with digital transformation. Upskilling involves training the current workforce to enhance their performance in existing roles, while reskilling means equipping staff with new skills for different organizational roles. Both approaches are essential to ensure that the workforce remains agile and responsive to changing business needs. Human resources play a crucial role in facilitating upskilling and reskilling initiatives. HR departments must identify organizational skills gaps and develop targeted training programs to address these needs. This may involve partnering with external training providers, implementing e-learning platforms, and fostering a culture of continuous improvement and lifelong learning (Bersin 2017).

Leadership is the backbone for driving workforce transformations and ensuring the successful adoption of digital technologies. Leaders need to have a vision for the future of work and effectively communicate this vision to employees. They should cultivate an environment that encourages experimentation, innovation, and continuous skill development (Brynjolfsson, McAfee 2014). In addition to providing strategic direction, leaders must be empathetic and supportive, recognizing the challenges employees may face during the transition to new ways of working. By offering guidance, resources, and opportunities for growth, leaders help employees navigate the complexities of digital transformation and build a resilient, future-ready workforce (Kane et al. 2015a).

Digital transformation radically changes the roles and skills of employees, necessitating a corresponding redesign of the organization with investments in reskilling and upskilling. Human resources and leadership play critical roles in facilitating these transitions, ensuring that the workforce remains agile and capable of meeting the demands of the digital age. By embracing continuous learning and fostering a culture of innovation, organizations can successfully navigate the challenges of digital transformation and build a resilient, future-ready workforce.

This connection of evidence-based management (EBM) and management of meaning (MEM) looks paradoxical in the beginning. Principles of EBM are in the center of functionalistic and neopositivistic paradigm in management science, while MEM is concept rooted in interpretativistic and symbolic paradigm. However, it seems that this integration is necessary on the ground of digital transformation. Contemporary management practice and theory is bridging EBM and MEM because organizations, leaders, and managers are shaping meanings and symbolic sphere by the use of data, creating EBM reality. Brand management, social media communication, virtual reality, contemporary advertising, and also leadership creation are examples of data-based decisions in management that are oriented toward MEM, shaping the symbolic, cultural and mental perspectives of people and social groups.

EBM is a management process that uses relevant evidence and scientific principles to make better decisions. This approach underlines the importance of using data, facts, and empirical research for making informed decisions. In essence, EBM aims to improve the quality of managerial decisions based on credible and relevant evidence rather than intuition, anecdote, or tradition (Rousseau 2006).

The main principles of EBM could be summarized by four rules:

1 Use of Best Available Evidence: Seek and use the best available evidence from various sources, including scientific research, organizational data, professional experience, and stakeholder input. This ensures that decisions are based on a comprehensive understanding of the issues.
2 Decision Support Tools: Utilize decision support tools such as data analytics, statistical models, and systematic reviews to analyze and interpret evidence. These tools enhance the accuracy and reliability of decision-making processes.
3 Continuous Learning: Foster a culture of continuous learning and development. Managers should be committed to staying informed about the latest research and best practices in their field and be willing to adapt their approaches based on new evidence (Briner, Denyer, Rousseau 2009).
4 Critical Thinking: Engage in critical thinking by questioning assumptions, beliefs, and conventional wisdom. Stay in touch with new information, consider alternative perspectives, and give proper weight to the evidence before deciding on actions.

While EBM deals with objective evidence, the MEM focuses on subjective interpretations, narratives, and symbolism that impact organizational reality. Integrating both approaches can lead to a more thorough understanding of organizational dynamics and enhance the effectiveness of managerial practices (Gioia, Chittipeddi 1991). The process of MEM includes creating shared meaning, sensemaking and sensegiving, and cultural sensivity. Managers and leaders help shape and transmit meanings within their organization through storytelling, metaphors, and symbols to communicate organizational values, goals, and strategies. Process of sensemaking involves individuals giving meaning to complex and ambiguous issues. Managers support sensemaking by providing context, framing issues meaningfully, and helping employees understand the implications of their decisions and actions (Weick 1995). Similarly, process of sensegiving is transmissions of meaning by leaders, managers, or influencers in contemporary societies to followers or wider audience. The condition of successful sensegiving is absorbtion of meanings by followers or audience. Managers must be aware of the cultural context in which they operate and be sensitive to the diverse values, beliefs, and norms of their staff. This involves respecting cultural differences and adjusting communication styles to suit different cultural backgrounds.

Combining EBM with the MEM offers new cognitive perspectives and pragmatic benefits in management. The epistemological perspective is creating the new paradigm of Management in Digital Revolution that links the perspective of EBM (connected to functionalistic and neopositivistic paradigm) with MEM (rooted in interpretativistic and symbolic paradigm). The move from new epistemology of Management in Digital Revolution to methodology means integration of quantitative and qualitative methods (mixed approach). Flexible methodology, joining deep perspective with scientific rigour, means combination of advance research methods with ecosystem of digital tools using Big Data, AI, ML, and IoT. The paradigm shift in the management science of the Digital Revolution era integrates the EBM perspective with the MEM, resulting in several key advantages from both epistemological and methodological perspectives. By merging the objective, data-driven approach of EBM with the subjective, interpretative insights of MEM, management science fosters a more comprehensive understanding of organizational phenomena. This dual approach enriches the epistemological foundation, facilitating more nuanced theories and models. Combining EBM and MEM allows for a deeper understanding of both the tangible and intangible aspects of management. This epistemological integration supports the development of more robust and holistic management theories that consider both empirical evidence and human factors. Mixed methods approach brings researchers more understanding, and presition, at the same time. The integration of quantitative and qualitative methods enhances the rigour and depth of management research. This mixed approach leverages the strengths of both methodologies, providing a more complete picture of complex management issues. Employing a flexible methodology that includes advanced research methods and digital tools allows researchers to tackle a wider range of questions. This adaptability is crucial in addressing the dynamic and multifaceted nature of contemporary management challenges. The use of digital tools in research methodologies enhances data collection, analysis, and interpretation. Technologies like Big Data and AI provide powerful means to uncover patterns and insights that traditional methods might miss, thereby advancing the frontiers of management science.

This comprehensive approach ultimately strengthens the scientific foundation of management practice, fostering innovation and leading to more effective and relevant theories and models.

1 Better Decision-Making: The quality of managerial decisions can be improved by combining objective facts with subjective views. This holistic approach ensures that decisions are based on facts while embracing the human and cultural features of organizational life.
2 Enhanced Communication: Integrating these approaches enhances organizational communication by aligning evidence-based strategies with meaningful stories. This helps ensure that employees understand and buy into organizational decisions and initiatives.
3 Greater Employee Engagement: Addressing both the rational and emotional aspects of work promotes better employee engagement and commitment, leading to higher motivation and job satisfaction, which is reflected in overall organizational performance.
4 Adaptability and Resilience: Organizations integrating EBM with meaning management navigate changes and uncertainty more effectively. This integrated approach allows for more flexible and adaptive responses to emerging challenges and opportunities.

Integrating EBM with the MEM significantly enhances organizational effectiveness. Managers are empowered to make informed decisions, ensure better communication, and foster a more committed and engaged workforce. This comprehensive approach can ultimately lead to improved organizational performance and a better work environment.

19 Future Paradigm? Post-Human Management?

Post-human management is a developing management theory that explores the impacts of advanced technologies on organizational practices, structures, and strategies. It investigates how technologies such as artificial intelligence (AI), robotics, and biotechnology are transforming human roles in the workplace and how managers can navigate this new landscape. Post-human management seeks to address the challenges and opportunities presented by these technologies (Pepperell 2003).

Post-human areas of management are wide, growing, and bringing new challenges both for theory and for practice of management.

- Human-Machine Collaboration: As AI and robotics become integrated into the workplace, effective human-machine collaboration is essential. Managers must balance human strengths like intuition and creativity with the precision and efficiency of machines. This involves designing workflows and processes that leverage the capabilities of both humans and machines to achieve optimal outcomes (Brynjolfsson, McAfee 2014).
- Ethical and Social Implications: The rise of advanced technologies raises important ethical and social questions. Post-human management involves addressing issues such as job displacement, privacy concerns, and the ethical use of AI and biotechnology. Managers must navigate these challenges by developing policies and practices that promote ethical behaviour and social responsibility (Floridi et al. 2018).
- Redefining Work and Roles: Advanced technologies are redefining traditional job roles and responsibilities. Post-human management requires rethinking how work is organized and what skills are needed in this new era. This may involve reskilling and upskilling employees to ensure they can thrive in a technology-driven environment (Manyika et al. 2017).
- Enhancing Human Capabilities: Biotechnology and AI offer opportunities to enhance human capabilities, such as cognitive and physical abilities. Post-human management explores how these enhancements can be integrated

DOI: 10.4324/9781003530947-24

into the workplace to improve productivity and well-being, while considering the ethical implications (Bostrom, Sandberg 2009).

Post-human management will require a re-evaluation of traditional human roles within organizational theory. The integration of AI, robotics, and biotechnology will push researchers to reconsider the human-machine relationship, focusing on how machines can complement human capabilities and redefine the essence of work. The rise of advanced technologies in management will necessitate the development of new ethical paradigms. Epistemologically, this will challenge researchers to create frameworks that address privacy concerns, job displacement, and the ethical use of AI and biotechnology, ensuring that technological advancements align with human values and social responsibilities. The methodological approach in post-human management will increasingly require interdisciplinary research, combining insights from fields such as cognitive science, robotics, ethics, and organizational behaviour. This integration will foster a more holistic understanding of how advanced technologies impact management practices. Methodologically, the adoption of AI and machine learning will transform research methods in management. Researchers will employ sophisticated data analytics and machine learning models to analyse large datasets, uncovering patterns and insights that were previously inaccessible. The future of post-human management research will likely involve experimental and simulation methods to explore human-machine interactions. Researchers will use simulations to model complex organizational scenarios and predict outcomes, providing a robust methodological framework for testing theories and hypotheses in a controlled environment. However, it could also lead to complexity level of research that could be very difficult or even impossible to understand by human cognitive capabilities. And, this is not only the problem of abilities of human brain but also cognitive capacities of social and research networks.

Managers play a crucial role in dealing with complexities of post-human management.

Managers must lead the integration of advanced technologies into the organization. This involves understanding the potential and limitations of these technologies and ensuring they are implemented in ways that align with the organization's goals and values. To thrive in a post-human era, organizations need a culture that embraces innovation and continuous improvement. Managers must cultivate an environment where employees feel empowered to experiment, take risks, and develop new ideas. As technology blurs the lines between human and machine, managers must develop ethical frameworks to guide decision-making. This includes establishing clear guidelines for the use of AI and biotechnology and ensuring these practices uphold the organization's ethical standards (Floridi et al. 2018). The transition to a post-human workplace can be challenging for employees. Managers must support their teams through this transition by providing training, resources, and emotional support. This helps employees adapt to new technologies and ensures they feel valued and supported (Kane et al. 2015a). Post-human management represents a significant shift in how organizations operate, driven by the integration of advanced technologies. Managers must navigate this new landscape by balancing human and machine capabilities, addressing ethical and social implications, redefining work roles, and enhancing human potential. By leading technological integration, fostering a culture of innovation, developing ethical frameworks, and supporting employee adaptation, managers can successfully guide their organizations into the post-human era.

References

Abner G.B., Kim S.Y., Perry J.L. (2017) Building evidence for public human resource management: Using middle range theory to link theory and data. *Review of Public Personnel Administration*, 37(2), 139–159.

Abubakar A.M., Elrehail H., Alatailat M.A., Elçi A. (2019) Knowledge management, decision-making style and organizational performance. *Journal of Innovation & Knowledge*, 4(2), 104–114.

Agrawal A., Gans J., Goldfarb A. (2018) *Prediction machines: The simple economics of artificial intelligence*. Harvard Business Review Press, Boston.

Al Saifi S.A. (2015) Positioning organisational culture in knowledge management research. *Journal of Knowledge Management*, 19(2), 164–189.

Aldag R.J., Stearns T.M. (1995) *Management*. South-Western Publishing Co., Cincinnati, OH.

Alsem K.J., Kostelijk E. (2008) Identity based marketing: A new balanced marketing paradigm. *European Journal of Marketing*, 42(9–10), 907–914.

Alvesson M. (2003) Beyond neopositivists, romantics, and localists: A reflexive approach to interviews in organizational research. *Academy of Management Review*, 28(1), 13–33.

Alvesson M., Deetz S. (2005) Critical theory and postmodernizm: Approaches to organization studies [w:] C. Grey, H. Willmott (red.), *Critical management studies. A reader* (pp. 255–283). Oxford University Press, New York.

Alvesson M., Hardy C., Harley B. (2008) Reflecting on reflexivity: Reflexive textual practices in organization and management theory. *Journal of Management Studies*, 45(3), 480–501.

Alvesson M., Willmott H. (red.) (1992) *Critical management studies*. SAGE, London.

Alvesson M., Willmott H. (1996) *Making sense of management. A critical introduction*. SAGE, London.

Alvesson M., Willmott H. (red.) (2003) *Studying management critically*. SAGE, London.

Andres P., Dobrovská D. (2015) Dilemmas of student technical and social science thinking [w:] *International conference on interactive collaborative learning (ICL)*, Firenze, Italy [online], doi: 10.1109/ICL.2015.7317986.

Ashcraft K.L. (2016) Fringe benefits? Revisi(ti)ng the relationship between feminism and critical management studies [w:] A. Prasad, P. Prasad, A.J. Mills, J.H. Mills (red.), *The Routledge companion to critical management studies* (pp. 93–106). Routledge, Abingdon.

Åsvoll H. (2014) Abduction, deduction and induction: can these concepts be used for an understanding of methodological processes in interpretative case studies? *International Journal of Qualitative Studies in Education*, 27(3), 289–307.

Bacharach S.B. (1989) Organizational theories: Some criteria for evaluation. *Academy of Management Review*, 14(4), 496–515.

Badea M. (2013) Cultural influences in human resources management. *Review of General Management*, 17(1), 179–187.

Baker, T., Smith, L. (2019) Educ-AI-Tion Rebooted? Exploring the Future of Artificial Intelligence in Schools and Colleges. https://www.nesta.org.uk/report/education-rebooted/

Barney J.B. (1995) Beyond individual methaphors in understanding how firms behave: A comment on game theory and prospect theory models of firm behavior [w:] R.P. Rumelt, D.E. Schendel, D.J. Teece (red.), *Fundamentals issues in strategy. A research agenda* (pp. 411–438). Harvard Business School Press, Boston, MA.

Barry D. (1996) Artful inquiry: A symbolic constructivist approach to social science research. *Qualitative Inquiry*, 2(4), 78–83.

Barton D., Court D., Elzinga D. (2012) Making advanced analytics work for you. *Harvard Business Review*, 90(10), 78–83.

Basole R.C., Rouse W.B., McGinnis L., Bodner D.A., Kessler W.C. (2011) Models of complex enterprise networks. *Journal of Enterprise Transformation*, 1(3), 208–230.

Becker H.S. (2003) The politics of presentation: Goffman and total institutions. *Symbolic Interaction*, 26(4), 659–669.

Benoit D.F. (2019) Real-time big data analytics: Framework and applications. *Journal of Big Data*, 6(1), 1–27.

Bersin J. (2017) *The future of work: It's already here*. Deloitte Insights, New York.

Bessen J. (2019) AI and jobs: The role of demand. NBER Working Paper No. 24235.

Besson P., Rowe F. (2012) Strategizing information systems-enabled organizational transformation: A transdisciplinary review and new directions. *Journal of Strategic Information Systems*, 21(2), 103–124.

Bhatt G.D. (2001) Knowledge management in organizations: Examining the interaction between technologies, techniques, and people. *Journal of Knowledge Management*, 5(1), 68–75.

Bielski M. (1996) *Organizacje: istota, struktury, procesy*. Wydawnictwo Uniwersytetu Łódzkiego, Łódź.

Binns R. (2018) Fairness in machine learning: Lessons from political philosophy. In *Proceedings of the 2018 conference on fairness, accountability, and transparency* (pp. 149–159). New York.

Bluhm D.J., Harman W., Lee T.W., Mitchell T.R. (2011) Qualitative research in management: A decade of progress. *Journal of Management Studies*, 48(8), 1866–1891.

Boell S.K., Cecez-Kecmanovic D. (2010) Literature reviews and the hermeneutic circle. *Australian Academic & Research Libraries*, 41(2), 129–144.

Bolman L.G., Deal T.E. (2003) *Reframing organisations. Artistry, choice and leadership*. Jossey-Bass, San Francisco, CA.

Bostrom N., Sandberg A. (2009) Cognitive enhancement: Methods, ethics, regulatory challenges. *Science and Engineering Ethics,* 15, 311–341. https://doi.org/10.1007/s11948-009-9142-5

Bourdieu P. (1987) Espace social et pouvoir symbolique [w:] P. Bourdieu (red.), *Choses dites* (pp. 223–266). Minuit, Paris.

Brewis J., Wray-Bliss E. (2008) Re-searching ethics: Towards a more reflexive critical management studies. *Organization Studies*, 29(12), 1521–1540.

Briner R.B., Denyer D., Rousseau D.M. (2009) Evidence-based management: Concept cleanup time? *Academy of Management Perspectives*, 23(4), 19–32.

Brown B. (2019) Agile transformation: Structures, processes, and mindsets for the digital age. *McKinsey Quarterly*.

Brunson N. (2006) *Mechanisms of hope: Maintaining the dream of the rational organization*. Copenhagen Business School Press, Copenhagen.

Brunson N. (2007) *The consequences of decision-making*. Oxford University Press, Oxford.

Brynjolfsson E., McAfee A. (2014) *The second machine age: Work, progress, and prosperity in a time of brilliant technologies*. W. W. Norton & Company, New York.

Brynjolfsson E., McAfee A. (2017) The business of artificial intelligence: What it can—and cannot—Do for your organization. *Harvard Business Review*, 7, 3–11.

Burrell G., Morgan G. (1979) *Sociological paradigms and organizational analysis*. Heinemann Books, London.

Calás M., Smircich L. (1991) Voicing seduction to silence leadership. *Organization Studies*, 12(4), 567–601.

Carroll S.J., Gillen D.I. (1987) Are the classical management functions useful in describing managerial work? *Academy of Management Review*, 12(1), 38–51.

Cassell C., Radcliffe L., Malik F. (2020) Participant reflexivity in organizational research design. *Organizational Research Methods*, 23(4), 750–773.

Chen H., Chiang R.H.L., Storey V.C. (2012) Business intelligence and analytics: From big data to big impact. *MIS Quarterly*, 36(4), 1165–1188.

Chui M., Löffler M., Roberts R. (2010) The internet of things. *McKinsey Quarterly*.

Cigoli V., Scabini E. (2012) The systemic paradigm: The intersubjective–narrative approach versus the relational–generational one [w:] L. L'Abate (red.), *Paradigms in theory construction* (pp. 217–234). Springer, New York.

Clegg S., Hardy C. (1997) Relativity without relativism: Reflexivity in post-paradigm organization studies. *British Journal of Management*, 8(2), 5–17.

Clegg S.R., Kornberger M. (2003) Modernism, postmodernism, management and organization theory [w:] Bingley (red.), *Post modernism and management* (pp. 57–88). Emerald Group Publishing Limited.

Colarelli S.M. (2003) *No best way: An evolutionary perspective on human resource management*. Praeger, Greenwich.

Coleman J.S. (1974) *Power and structure of society*. WW Norton & Company, New York.

Cronen V., Pearce, B. (eds.) (1988). Coordinated management of meaning: A critical theory. International and Intercultural Communication Annual, 12, 66–98.

Cunliffe A.L. (2011) Crafting qualitative research: Morgan and Smircich 30 years on. *Organizational Research Methods*, 14(4), 647–673.

Daellenbach H., McNickle D., Dye S. (2012) *Management science: Decision-making through systems thinking*. Macmillan International Higher Education, New York.

Dahredorf R. (1969) *Class and class conflict in industrial society*. London, Routledge.

Davenport T.H. (2014) *Big data at work: Dispelling the myths, uncovering the opportunities*. Harvard Business Review Press, Watertown, MA, USA.

Davenport T.H., Harris J.G. (2007) *Competing on analytics: The new science of winning*. Harvard Business Review Press, Watertown, MA, USA.

Davenport T.H., Kirby J. (2016) *Only humans need apply: Winners and losers in the age of smart machines*. Harper Business, New York.
Davenport T.H., Ronanki R. (2018) Artificial intelligence for the real world. *Harvard Business Review*, 96(1), 108–116.
Davenport T.H., Westerman G. (2018) Why so many high-profile digital transformations fail. *Harvard Business Review*, Watertown, MA, USA.
De Dreu C.K., Gross J. (2019) Homo oeconomicus with a personality–trait-based differences in decision making [w:] A. Schram, A. Ule (red.), *Handbook of research methods and applications in experimental economics*. Edward Elgar, Cheltenham.
De Moya J.F., Pallud J. (2020) From panopticon to heautopticon: A new form of surveillance introduced by quantified-self practices. *Information Systems Journal*, 30(6), 940–976.
Deal T.E., Kennedy A.A. (1988) *Corporate cultures: The rites and rituals of corporate life*. Penguin Books, Harmondsworth.
Deal T.E., Kennedy A.A. (1982) *Corporate Cultures. Reading*. Addison-Wesley, MA.
Deetz S. (1995) *Transforming communication, transforming business: Building responsive and responsible workplaces*. Cresskill, Hapton.
Deleuze G., Guattari F. (2004) *Anti-Oedipus*, trans. R. Hurley, M. Seem, H.R. Lane. Continuum, London, New York.
Denison D. (1996) What is the difference between organizational culture and organizational climate? A native's point of view on a decade of paradigm wars. *The Academy of Management Review*, 21(3), 619–654.
Denzin N. (1970) *The Research Act: Theorethical introduction to sociological methods*. Aldine Publishing Company, Chicago, IL.
Dixon J., Dogan R. (2002) Towards constructive corporate governance: From 'certainties' to a plurality principle. *Philosophy of Management. Formerly Reason in Practice*, 2(3), 51–71.
Donaldson J., Fafaliou I. (2007) Principles of administration revisited. *International Journal of Social Economics*, 34(5), 297–309.
Donaldson L. (1995) *American anti-management theories of organization: A critique of paradigm proliferation*, vol. 25. Cambridge University Press, Cambridge.
Donovan R.J., Henley N. (2003) *Social marketing: Principles and practice*. IP Communications, Melbourne.
Doppelt G. (2013) Explaining the success of science: Kuhn and scientific realists. *Topoi*, 32(1), 43–51.
Dubin R. (1983) Theory building in applied areas [w:] M.D. Dunnette (red.), *Handbook of industrial and organizational psychology* (pp. 93–138). John Wiley, New York.
Eagleton-Pierce M., Knafo S. (2020) Introduction: The political economy of managerialism. *Review of International Political Economy*, 27(4), 763–779.
Eckhardt G.M., Dholakia N., Varman R. (2013) Ideology for the 10 billion: Introduction to globalization of marketing ideology. *Journal of Macromarketing*, 33(1), 7–12.
Einarsen S. (1999) The nature and causes of bullying at work. *International Journal of Manpower*, 20(1/2), 16–27.
Ewoldsen D.R. (2017) Normal science and paradigm shift [w:] *The international encyclopedia of communication research methods* [online]. John Wiley & Sons, Inc., doi: 10.1002/9781118901731.iecrm0169.

Feyerabend P. (1975) *Against method*. NLB, London.

Feyerabend, P. (1993). *Against Method* (3rd ed.). London and New York: Verso.

Fitzgerald M., Kruschwitz N., Bonnet D., Welch M. (2014) Embracing digital technology: A new strategic imperative. *MIT Sloan Management Review*, 55(2), 1–12.

Fleck L. (1986) Crisis in science [w:] T. Schnelle & R. S. Cohen (red.), *Cognition and fact. Boston studies in the philosophy of science*, vol. 87, (pp. 153–158). Springer, Dordrecht.

Fleming P., Spicer A. (2014) Power in management and organization science. *Academy of Management Annals*, 8(1), 237–298 .

Floridi L. (2019) *The logic of information: A theory of philosophy as conceptual design*. Oxford University Press, Oxford.

Floridi L., Cowls J., King T.C., Taddeo M. (2018) How to design AI for social good: Seven essential factors. *Science and Engineering Ethics*, 24(5), 1–16.

Fournier V., Grey C. (2000) At the critical moment: Conditions and prospects for critical management studies. *Human Relations*, 53(1), 7–32.

Frenkel M., Shenhav Y. (2006) From binarism back to hybridity: A postcolonial reading of management and organization studies. *Organization Studies*, 27(6), 855–876.

Fuat Firat A., Venkatesh A. (1993) Postmodernity: The age of marketing. *International Journal of Research in Marketing*, 10(3), 227–249.

Fukuyama F. (2001) Social capital, civil society and development. *Third World Quarterly*, 22, 7–20. https://doi.org/10.1080/713701144.

Gartner (2020) *The future of work requires a relearning revolution*. Gartner Research, Stamford, Connecticut.

Gazheli A., Antal M., van den Bergh J. (2015) The behavioral basis of policies fostering long-run transitions: Stakeholders, limited rationality and social context. *Futures*, 69, 14–30.

Gendron Y. (2018) On the elusive nature of critical (accounting) research. *Critical Perspectives on Accounting*, 50(C), 1–12.

Gherardi S. (2003) Feminist theory and organization theory: A dialogue on new bases [w:] C. Knudsen, H. Tsoukas (red.), *The Oxford handbook of organization theory* (pp. 127–132). Oxford University Press, Oxford.

Gioia D.A., Pitre E. (1990) Multi-paradigm perspective on theory building. *The Academy of Management Review*, 15(4), 584–602.

Gioia D.A., Chittipeddi K. (1991) Sensemaking and sensegiving in strategic change initiation. *Strategic Management Journal*, 12(6), 433–448.

Gladwell M. (2005) *Blink: The power of thinking without thinking*. Back Bay Books, Little, Brown, New York.

Goffee R., Jones G. (1998) *The character of a corporation*. Harper Collins Publishers, New York.

Goh S.C., Richards G. (1997) Benchmarking the learning capability of organizations. *European Management Journal*, 15(5), 575–583.

Goldman G.A. (2016) Multiparadigmatic, cooperative opportunities for the study of business management. *Management Dynamics*, 25(3), 2–15.

Gouldner A. (1970) *The coming crisis of Western sociology*. Basic Books, New York.

Grey C. (1996) Towards a critique of managerialism: The contribution of Simone Weil. *Journal of Management Studies*, 33(5), 591–612.

Gulati R., Puranam P., Tushman M. (2012) Meta-organization design: Rethinking design in interorganizational and community contexts. *Strategic Management Journal*, 33(6), 571–586.

Gummson E. (1991) *Qualitative methods in management research*. SAGE Publications, Newbury Park.

Haldin-Herrgard T. (2000) Difficulties in diffusion of tacit knowledge in organizations. *Journal of Intellectual Capital*, 1(4), 357–365.

Handy C. (1985) *Understanding Organisations*. (4th ed.). Penguin Books, New York.

Hambrick D.C., Chen M.J. (2008) New academic fields as admittance-seeking social movements: The case of strategic management. *Academy of Management Review*, 33(1), 32–54.

Haraway D. (1990) *Primate visions: Gender race and nature in the word of modern science*. Routledge, London.

Harding N. (2003) *The social construction of management*. Routledge, London.

Harding S. (1986) *The science question in feminism*. Open University Press, Buckingham.

Hardt M., Negri A. (2001) *Empire*. Harvard University Press, Cambrige, London.

Harney S., Dunne S. (2013) More than nothing? Accounting, business, and management studies, and the research audit. *Critical Perspectives on Accounting*, 24(4–5), 338–349.

Harris K.L. (2016) Feminist dilemmatic theorizing: New materialism in communication studies. *Communication Theory*, 26(2), 150–170.

Haselton M.G., Buss D.M. (2004) Error management theory: A new perspective on biases in cross-sex mind reading [w:] D.T. Kenrick, C.L. Luce (red.), *The functional mind. Readings in evolutionary psychology* (pp. 81–91). Pearson, Boston, MA.

Hassard J., Wolfram Cox J. (2013) Can sociological paradigms still inform organizational analysis? A paradigm model for post-paradigm times. *Organization Studies*, 34(11), 1701–1728.

Hatch M.J. (1997) Irony and the social construction of contradiction in the humor of a management team. *Organization Studies*, 8(3), 275–288.

Hatch M.J., Schultz M. (1996) Living with multiple paradigms. The case of paradigm interplay in organizational culture studies. *Academy of Management Review*, 21(2), 529–557.

Hatch M.J., Schultz M. (red.) (2004) *Organizational identity*. Oxford University Press, Oxford.

Hatch M.J. & Schultz M. (2000) Scaling the Tower of Babel: Relational differences between identity, image and culture in organizations [w:] M. Schultz, M.J. Hatch, M.H. Larsen, (red.), The Expressive Organization, pp. 11–36. Oxford University Press, Oxford.

Hibbert P., Sillince J., Diefenbach T., Cunliffe A.L. (2014) Relationally reflexive practice: A generative approach to theory development in qualitative research. *Organizational Research Methods*, 17(3), 278–298.

Hines S. (2019) The feminist frontier: On trans and feminism. *Journal of Gender Studies*, 28(2), 145–157.

Hitt M.A. (1997) The maturation of the Academy of Management Journal. *Academy of Management Journal*, 40(6), 1450–1455.

Hodgson B. (2007) *Logical positivism and the Vienna circle. BOUNDAS, CV the Edinburgh companion to twentieth century philosophies*. Edinburgh University Press Ltd., Edinburgh.

Hofmann E. (2017) Big data and supply chain decisions: The impact of volume, variety and velocity properties on the bullwhip effect. *International Journal of Production Research*, 55(17), 5108–5126.

Hofstede G. (1984) *Culture's consequences*. SAGE Publications, Beverly Hills, CA.

Holbrook M.B. (1995) The three faces of elitism: Postmodernism, political correctness, and popular culture. *Journal of Macromarketing*, 15, 128–165.

Holmwood J. (2005) Functionalism and its critics [w:] A. Harrington (red.), *Modern social theory: An introduction* (pp. 87–109). Oxford University Press, Oxford.

Holsapple C.W. (1995) Knowledge management in decision making and decision support. *Knowledge and Policy*, 8(1), 5–22.

Howcroft D., Trauth E. (2005) *Handbook of critical information systems research*. Edward Elger, London.

Huang M.H., Rust R.T. (2018) Artificial intelligence in service. *Journal of Service Research*, 21(2), 155–172.

Hudon P.A., Rouillard C. (2015) Critical management studies and public administration: Reinterpreting democratic governance using critical theory and poststructuralism. *Canadian Public Administration*, 58(4), 527–548.

Hyötyläinen R. (2000) *Development mechanisms of strategic enterprise networks: Learning and innovation in networks*. VTT Technical Research Centre of Finland, Espoo.

Iansiti M., Lakhani K.R. (2017) The truth about blockchain. *Harvard Business Review*, 95(1), 118–127.

Jackson M. (2003) *Systems thinking: Creative holism for managers*. Wiley John & Sons Ltd, Hoboken, New Jersey.

Jacques R. (1996) *Manufacturing the employee: Management knowledge from the 19th to 21st centuries*. SAGE Publications, London.

Janićijević N. (2011) Methodological approaches in the research of organizational culture. *Economic Annals*, 56(189), 69–99.

Johnson P., Duberley J. (2003) Reflexivity in management research. *Journal of Management Studies*, 40(5), 1279–1303.

Johnson P., Duberley J. (2015) Inductive praxis and management research: Towards a reflexive framework. *British Journal of Management*, 26(4), 760–776.

Kadirov D., Varey R.J. (2011) Symbolism in marketing systems. *Journal of Macromarketing*, 31(2), 160–171.

Kane G.C., Palmer D., Phillips A.N., Kiron D. (2015a). Is cybersecurity the most significant barrier to digital transformation? *MIT Sloan Management Review*. Available at https://sloanreview.mit.edu/projects/strategy-drivesdigital-transformation/

Kane G.C., Palmer D., Phillips A.N., Kiron D., Buckley N. (2015b). Strategy, not technology, drives digital transformation. *MIT Sloan Management Review*, 14(1), 1–25.

Kantola J., Squires J. (2012) From state feminism to market feminism? *International Political Science Review*, 33(4), 382–400.

Keller E.F. (1993) *Secrets of life, secrets of heath. Essays on gender, language and science*. Routledge, London.

Khorasani S.T., Almasifard M. (2017) Evolution of management theory within 20 century: A systemic overview of paradigm shifts in management. *International Review of Management and Marketing*, 7(3), 134–137.

Kingsbury N., Scanzoni J. (2009) Structural-functionalism [w:] P. Boss, W.J. Doherty, R. LaRossa, W.R. Schumm, S.K. Steinmetz (red.), *Sourcebook of family theories and methods* (pp. 195–221). Springer, Boston, MA.

Kirchgässner G. (2008) *Homo oeconomicus: The economic model of behaviour and its applications in economics and other social sciences*, seria The European Heritage in Economics and the Social Sciences, vol. 6. Springer Science & Business Media, Cham.

Kirchner S. (2013) How organizations become enduring: Disentangling the organizational identity paradox [w:] J. Sydow, G. Schreyögg (red.), *Self-reinforcing processes in and among organizations* (pp. 35–54). Palgrave Macmillan, London.

Koontz H. (1961) The management theory jungle. *Journal of the Academy of Management*, 4(3), 174–188.

Koss Hartmann R. (2014) Subversive functionalism: For a less canonical critique in critical management studies. *Human Relations*, 67(5), 611–632.

Kotter J.P. (1996) *Leading change*. Harvard Business Review Press, Boston.

Kramarae C. (1981) *Women and men speaking: Frameworks for analysis*. Newbury House, Rowley, MA.

Kuhn T.S. (2012) *The structure of scientific revolutions*. University of Chicago Press, Chicago, IL.

Lamar M.R., Helm H.M. (2017) Understanding the researcher identity development of counselor education and supervision doctoral students. *Counselor Education and Supervision*, 56(1), 2–18.

Laney D. (2001) *3D data management: Controlling data volume, velocity, and variety*. META Group Research Note.

Landes DS. (2000) *Bogactwo i nędza narodów. Dlaczego jedni są tak bogaci, a inni lak ubodzy*, Muza, Warszawa.

Laszlo C., Waddock S., Sroufe R. (2017) Torn between two paradigms: A struggle for the soul of business schools. *AI Practitioner*, 19(2), 1–4.

Laureiro-Martínez D., Brusoni S. (2018) Cognitive flexibility and adaptive decision-making: Evidence from a laboratory study of expert decision makers. *Strategic Management Journal*, 39(4), 1031–1058.

Lawrence P.R., Pirson M. (2015) Economistic and humanistic narratives of leadership in the age of globality: Toward a renewed Darwinian theory of leadership. *Journal of Business Ethics*, 128(2), 383–394.

Lee C.Y. (2012) Korean culture and its influence on business practice in South Korea. *The Journal of International Management Studies*, 7(2), 184–191.

Lee J., Kao H.A., Yang S. (2014) Service innovation and smart analytics for industry 4.0 and big data environment. *Procedia CIRP*, 16, 3–8.

Lengnick-Hall M.L., Lengnick-Hall C.A., Andrade L.S., Drake B. (2009) Strategic human resource management: The evolution of the field. *Human Resource Management Review*, 19(2), 64–85.

Lennon K. (2004) Feminist epistemology [w:] I. Niiniluoto, M. Sintonen, J. Woleński (red.), *Handbook of epistemology* (pp. 1013–1026). Kluwer Academic Publishers, Dordrecht, Boston, MA, London.

Leydesdorff L. (2021) Evolutionary and institutional triple helix models [w:] L. Leydesdorff (red.), *The evolutionary dynamics of discursive knowledge* (pp. 1–247). Springer, Cham.

Lips-Wiersma M., Morris L. (2009) Discriminating between 'meaningful work' and the 'management of meaning'. *Journal of Business Ethics*, 88(3), 491–511.

Longino H. (2001) *The fate of knowledge*. Princeton University Press, Princeton, NJ.

Longino H.E. (2017) Feminist epistemology [w:] J. Greco, E. Sosa (red.), *The Blackwell guide to epistemology* (pp. 325–353). Blackwell Publishing, Malden, MA.

Love P.E., Holt G.D., Li H. (2002) Triangulation in construction management research. *Engineering Construction and Architectural Management*, 9(4), 294–303.

Makridakis S. (2017) The forthcoming Artificial Intelligence (AI) revolution: Its impact on society and firms. *Futures*, 90, 46–60.

Mancosu P. (1998) *From Brouwer to Hilbert, the debate on the foundations of mathematics in the 1920's*. Oxford University Press, New York.

Manyika J., Chui M., Brown B., Bughin J., Dobbs R., Roxburgh C., Byers A.H. (2011) *Big data: The next frontier for innovation, competition, and productivity*. McKinsey Global Institute, Washington.

Manyika J., Chui M., Miremadi M., Bughin J., George K., Willmott P., Dewhurst M. (2017) *A future that works: Automation, employment, and productivity*. McKinsey Global Institute, Washington.

Martin J. (2002) *Organizational culture. Mapping the terrain*. SAGE, Thousand Oaks, CA, London.

Martinez F., Peattie K., Vazquez-Brust D. (2021) Faith in the future: On a mission to integrate sustainability into management theory and practice. *Futures*, 125, 1–25.

Maylor H., Turner N. (2017) Understand, reduce, respond: Project complexity management theory and practice. *International Journal of Operations & Production Management*, 37(8), 1076–1093.

McAfee A., Brynjolfsson E. (2012) Big data: The management revolution. *Harvard Business Review*, 90(10), 60–68.

McKelvey B. (2003) Postmodernism versus truth in management theory [w:] E.A. Locke (red.), *Post modernism and management (research in the sociology of organizations, vol. 21)* (pp. 57–88). Emerald Group Publishing Limited, London.

Melé D., Cantón C.G. (2014) The idea of the human person in management and organizational theories [w:] Domènec Melé, César González Canton (red.), *Human foundations of management* (pp. 30–49). IESE Business Collection, Palgrave Macmillan, London.

Micklethwait J., Wooldridge A. (2000) *The world tomorrow: The essentials of globalization*. Times Books, New York.

Mintzberg H. (1991) A letter to Maria Calás and Linda Smircich. *Organization Studies*, 12(4), 602–602.

Mintzberg H. (1980) Structure in 5's: A synthesis of the research on organization design. *Management Science*, 26(3), 322–341.

Mir R., Watson A. (2000) Strategic management and the philosophy of science: The case for a constructivist methodology. *Strategic Management Journal*, 21(9), 941–953.

Mitchell A. (2018) A review of mixed methods, pragmatism, and abduction techniques [w:] P. Demartini, M. Marchiori (red.), *Proceedings of the 17th European conference on research methods for business & management studies*. Università Roma TRE, Rome, 12–13 lipca 2018, ACPI.

Monin N. (2004) *Management theory. A critical and reflective reading*. Routledge, London, New York.

Morgan G. (1998) *Images of organization:* The executive edition. SAGE Publications, Thousand Oaks, CA.

Nicolini D. (2012) *Practice theory, work, and organization: An introduction*. Oxford University Press, Oxford.

Norris J., Sawyer R.D. (2012) Toward a dialogic methodology [w:] J. Norris, R.D. Sawyer, D. Lund (red.), *Duoethnography: Dialogic methods for social, health, and educational research* (pp. 9–39). Left Coast Press, Walnut Creek, California.

O'Donovan G. (2006) *The corporate culture handbook. How to plan, implement and measure a successful culture change programme*. The Liffey Press, Dublin.

Oakley A. (2000) *Experiments in knowing. Gender and method in the social sciences*. The New Press, New York.

Outhwaite R.W. (2015) Positivism, sociological [w:] James D. Wright (red.), *International encyclopedia of the social and behavioral sciences: Second edition* (pp. 625–629). Elsevier, Oxford.

Papadakis V.M., Lioukas S., Chambers D. (1998) Strategic decision-making processes: The role of management and context. *Strategic Management Journal*, 19(2), 115–147.

Parker S., Parker M. (2017) Antagonism, accommodation and agonism in critical management studies: Alternative organizations as allies. *Human Relations*, 70(11), 1366–1387.

Peaucelle J.L. (2000) From Taylorism to post-Taylorism: Simultaneously pursuing several management objectives. *Journal of Organizational Change Management*, 13(5), 452–467.

Pepperell R. (2003) *The post-human condition: Consciousness beyond the brain*. Intellect Books, Bristol.

Peters T. (1994) *The Tom Peters seminar. Crazy times call for crazy organisations*. MacMillan, London.

Peticca-Harris A., McKenna S. (2013) Identity struggle, professional development and career: A career/life history of a human resource management professional. *Journal of Management Development*, 32(8), 823–835.

Pfeffer J. (2007) A modest proposal: How we might change the process and product of managerial research. *Academy of Management Journal*, 50(6), 1334–1345.

Philipsen K. (2018) Theory building: Using abductive search strategies [w:] Per Vagn Freytag Louise Young (red.), *Collaborative research design* (pp. 45–71). Springer, Singapore.

Pinker S. (2003) *The blank stale: The modern denial of human nature*. Penguin, New York.

Pinker S. (2004) Language as a adaptation on the cognitive niche [w:] D.T. Kenrick, C.L. Luce (red.), *The functional mind. Readings in evolutionary psychology* (pp. 16–37). Pearson, Boston, MA.

Pinnington A. (2001) Charles Handy: The exemplary guru. *Philosophy of Management. Formerly Reason in Practice*, 1(3), 47–55.

Pintelon L.M., Gelders L.F. (1992) Maintenance management decision making. *European Journal of Operational Research*, 58(3), 301–317.

Polanyi M. (1958) *Personal knowledge: Towards a post-critical philosophy*. London: Routledge & Kegan Paul.

Primecz H. (2020) Positivist, constructivist and critical approaches to international human resource management and some future directions. *German Journal of Human Resource Management*, 34(2), 124–147.

Pringle R. (2005) Sexuality at work [w:] C. Grey, H. Willmott (red.), *Critical management studies. A reader* (pp. 201–284). Oxford University Press, New York.

Pritchard D. (2002) Are economic decisions rational? Path dependence, lock-in and 'hinge' propositions. *Philosophy of Management. Formerly Reason in Practice*, 2(3), 29–40.

Pullen A., Vachhani S., Gagnon S., Cornelius N. (2017) Editorial: Critical diversity, philosophy and praxis. *Gender, Work and Organization*, 24(5), 451–456.

Rai A. (2020) Explainable AI: From black box to glass box. *Journal of the Academy of Marketing Science*, 48(1), 137–141.

Ravasi D., Schultz M. (2006) Responding to organizational identity threats: Exploring the role of organizational culture. *Academy of Management Journal*, 49(3), 433–458.

Remenyi D., Williams B., Money A., Swartz E. (2005) *Doing research in business and management. An introduction to process and method*. SAGE, London.

Ridder H.G., Hoon C. (2009) Introduction to the special issue: Qualitative methods in research on human resource management. *German Journal of Human Resource Management*, 23(2), 93–106.

Rinehart J. (2001) Transcending Taylorism and Fordism? Three decades of work restructuring [w:] R. Baldoz, C. Koeber, P. Kraft (red.), *The critical study of work: Labor, technology, and global production* (pp. 179–195). Temple University Press, Philadelphia.

Robertson B.J. (2015) *Holacracy: The new management system for a rapidly changing world*. Henry Holt and Co, New York.

Rorty R. (2007) *Philosophy as cultural politics: Philosophical papers volume 4*. Cambridge University Press, Cambridge.

Rorty, R. (1991) *Essays on Heidegger and others: Philosophical papers*. Cambridge University Press, New York.

Ross J.W., Beath C.M., Sebastian I.M. (2017) *Designed for digital: How to architect your business for sustained success*. MIT Press, Massachusetts.

Rousseau D.M. (2006) Is there such a thing as "evidence-based management"? *Academy of Management Review*, 31(2), 256–269.

Sage D., Dainty A., Brookes N. (2014) A critical argument in favor of theoretical pluralism: Project failure and the many and varied limitations of project management. *International Journal of Project Management*, 32(4), 544–555.

Saltelli A., Ravetz J., Funtowicz S. (2016) Who will solve the crisis in science [w:] A. Benessia, J.R. Ravetz, S. Funtowicz i in. (red.), *Science on the verge*, (pp. 1–30). Arizona State University, Arizona.

Sandberg W.R. (1992) Strategic management's potential contributions to a theory of entrepreneurship. *Entrepreneurship Theory and Practice*, 16(3), 73–90.

Sapru R.K. (2008) *Administrative theories and management thought*. PHI Learning Pvt. Ltd, Delhi.

Saren M., Svensson P. (2009) Marketing [w:] M. Alvesson, T. Bridgman, H. Willmott (red.), *The Oxford handbook of critical management studies* (pp. 371–391). Oxford University Press, Oxford.

Schein E.H. (1992) *Organizational culture and leadership*. Jossey-Bass, San Francisco, CA.

Scherer, K.R. (2009) The dynamic architecture of emotion: Evidence for the component process model. *Cognition and Emotion*, 23(7), 1307–1351.

Schmitt F.F. (1994) *Socializing epistemology*. Rowman & Littlefield, Lanham.

Schnackenberg A.K., Bundy J., Coen C.A., Westphal J.D. (2019) Capitalizing on categories of social construction: A review and integration of organizational research on symbolic management strategies. *Academy of Management Annals*, 13(2), 1–96.

Schwab K. (2017) *The fourth industrial revolution*. Crown Business, New York.

Shankaranarayanan G., Cai Y. (2006) Supporting data quality management in decision-making. *Decision Support Systems*, 42(1), 302–317.

Shaw E.H., Tamilia R.D. (2001) Robert Bartels and the history of marketing thought. *Journal of Macromarketing*, 21(2), 156–163.

Shi W., Cao J., Zhang Q., Li Y., Xu L. (2016) Edge computing: Vision and challenges. *IEEE Internet of Things Journal*, 3(5), 637–646.

Shrivastava P. (1986) Is strategic management ideological? *Journal of Management*, 12(3), 363–377.

Sim S. (2001) Postmodernism and philosophy [w:] S. Sim (red.), *The Routledge companion to postmodernism*. Routledge, New York.

Simon H.A. (1978) Rationality as process and as product of thought. *American Economic Review*, 68, 1–16.

Simon, H.A. (1991) Organizations and markets. *Journal of Economic Perspectives*, 5(2), 25–44.

Skålén P., Hackley C. (2011) Marketing-as-practice. Introduction to the special issue. *Scandinavian Journal of Management*, 27(2), 189–195.

Smircich L. (1983) Studing organisations as cultures [w:] G. Morgan (red.), *Beyond method: Strategies for social research* (pp. 160–172). Beverly Hills, London, New Delhi.

Soelberg P. (1966) Unprogrammed decision making. *Academy of Management Proceedings*, 1966(1), 3–16.

Sokal A.D. (1996) Transgressing the boundairies: Towards a transformative hermeneutics of quantum gravity. *Social Text*, 46/47, 217–252.

Spicer A., Alvesson M., Kärreman D. (2009) Critical performativity: The unfinished business of critical management studies. *Human Relations*, 62(4), 537–560.

Spreitzer G.M. (1995) Psychological empowerment in the workplace: Dimensions, measurement, and validation. *Academy of Management Journal*, 38(5), 1442–1465.

Spreitzer G.M., Cameron L., Garrett L. (2017) Alternative work arrangements: Two images of the new world of work. *Annual Review of Organizational Psychology and Organizational Behavior*, 4(1), 473–499.

Suk-Young Chwe M. (2001) *Rational ritual. Culture, coordination and common knowledge*. Princeton University Press, Princeton, NJ and Oxford.

Sułkowski Ł. (2015) Management – From epistemology by methodology to social practice of academia cognitive challenges in management science 2. *Przedsiębiorczość i Zarządzanie*, 16(2), 111–119.

Sułkowski Ł. (2016) The development of post-academic cultures in higher education institutions [w:] J. Teczke (red.), *State, society and business–Development of contemporary management* (pp. 167–176). Wydawnictwo International Management Fundation, Cracow University of Economics, Cracow, Saint Petersburg.

Swedberg R. (1990) *Economics and sociology: Redefining their boundaries: Conversations with economists and sociologists*. Princeton University Press, Princeton, NJ.

Sweeney E.P., Hardaker G. (1994) The importance of organisational and national culture. *European Business Review*, 94(5), 3–14.

Swennen A., Jones K., Volman M. (2010) Teacher educators: Their identities, sub-identities and implications for professional development. *Professional Development in Education*, 36(1–2), 131–148.

Tankard C. (2012) Big data security. *Network Security*, 2012(7), 5–8.
Tao F., Zhang H., Liu A., Nee A.Y.C. (2019) Digital twin in industry: State-of-the-art. *IEEE Transactions on Industrial Informatics*, 15(4), 2405–2415.
Thursfield D., Hamblett J. (2004) Human resource management and realism: A morphogenetic approach [w:] S. Fleetwood, S. Ackroyd (red.), *Critical realist applications in organisation and management studies* (pp. 113–130). Routledge, New York.
Touraine A. (1978) *La voix et le regard*, Seuil, Paris.
Tronvoll B., Brown S.W., Gremler D.D., Edvardsson B. (2011) Paradigms in service research. *Journal of Service Management*, 22(5), 560–585.
Tushman M.L., Nadler D.A. (1978) Information processing as an integrating concept in organizational design. *Academy of Management Review*, 3(3), 613–624.
Van Heerde H., Helsen K., Dekimpe M.G. (2007) *The impact of a product-harm crisis on marketing effectiveness. Marketing Science*, 26(2), 230–245.
Verduijn K., Dey P., Tedmanson D., Essers C. (2014) Emancipation and/or oppression? Conceptualizing dimensions of criticality in entrepreneurship studies. *International Journal of Entrepreneurial Behaviour & Research*, 20(2), 98–107.
Vial G. (2019) Understanding digital transformation: A review and a research agenda. *Journal of Strategic Information Systems*, 28(2), 118–144.
Von Solms R., Van Niekerk J. (2013) From information security to cyber security. *Computers & Security*, 38, 97–102.
Walker H., Symon G., Davies B. (1996) Assessing organizational culture: A comparison of methods. *International Journal of Selection and Assessment*, 4, 96–105.
Weber M. (2002) Gospodarka i społeczeństwo: Zarys socjologii rozumiejącej. Warsaw: PWN.
Weick K. (1987) Substitutes for corporate strategy [w:] D. Teece (red.), *The competitive challenge* (pp. 22–33). Ballinger, Cambridge.
Weick K.E. (1979) *The social psychology of organizing*. Addison-Wesley, Reading, MA.
Weick K.E. (1995) *Sensemaking in organizations*. Sage Publications, Los Angeles.
Westerman G., Bonnet D., McAfee A. (2014) *Leading digital: Turning technology into business transformation*. Harvard Business Review Press, Harvard.
Wicks A.C., Freeman R.E. (1998) Organization studies and the new pragmatism: Positivism, anti-positivism, and the search for ethics. *Organization Science*, 9(2), 123–140.
Wilson H.J., Daugherty P.R. (2018) Collaborative intelligence: Humans and AI are joining forces. *Harvard Business Review*, 96(4), 114–123.
Wood J.T. (1997) *Communication theories in action*. Wadsworth, Belmont.
Wood M. (2012) Marketing social marketing. *Journal of Social Marketing*, 2(2), 94–102.
Workman Jr J.P., Homburg C., Gruner K. (1998) Marketing organization: An integrative framework of dimensions and determinants. *Journal of Marketing*, 62(3), 21–41.
Wright N., Losekoot E. (2012) Interpretative research paradigms: Points of difference [w:] *Proceedings of the 11th European conference on research methods in business management: ECRM 2012*. University of Bolton, Bolton, 28–29 czerwca 2012, Academic Publishing International.
Yi Y., Yongxia J.L.C. (2007) A literature review of the cognitive school in strategic management. *Nanjing Business Review*, 34(6), 156–160.
Zieleniewski J. (1976) *Organizacja zespołów ludzkich*. PWN, Warszawa.
Zsolnai L., Junghagen S., Tencati A. (2012) Redefining the roles and duties of management. *Journal of Global Responsibility*, 3(1), 121–133.

Index

Note: **Bold** page numbers refer to tables.

For Product Safety Concerns and Information please contact our EU representative GPSR@taylorandfrancis.com
Taylor & Francis Verlag GmbH, Kaufingerstraße 24, 80331 München, Germany

www.ingramcontent.com/pod-product-compliance
Ingram Content Group UK Ltd.
Pitfield, Milton Keynes, MK11 3LW, UK
UKHW022354190926
475702UK00015B/2288
9781032871028